THE RIDE DOWN

Arthur Miller (1915-2005) was b
and studied at the University of
My Sons (1947), *Death of a Salesman* (1949),
A View from the Bridge and *A Memory of Two Mondays* (1955),
After the Fall (1964), *Incident at Vichy* (1964), *The Price* (1968), *The
Creation of the World and Other Business* (1972), and *The American
Clock*. He has also written a novel, *Focus* (1945), *The Misfits*,
which was filmed in 1960, and the text for *In Russia* (1969),
Chinese Encounters (1979), and *In the Country* (1977), three books
of photographs by his wife, Inge Morath. Other works include
Salesman in Beijing (1984); *Danger: Memory!* (1987); *Timebends*, a
memoir (1988); *The Ride Down Mt. Morgan* (1991), *The Last
Yankee* (1993); and *Broken Glass* (1994), which won the 1995
Olivier Award for Best Play; and a novella, *Homely Girl, a Life*
(1995). Recent plays include *Mr. Peters' Connections, Resurrection
Blues,* and his last play *Finishing the Picture.* He was awarded the
Avery Hopwood Award for Playwriting at University of Michigan
in 1936. He twice won the New York Drama Critics Circle
Award, received two Emmy awards and three Tony Awards for
his plays, as well as a Tony Award for Lifetime Achievement. He
also won an Obie award, a BBC Best Play Award, the George
Foster Peabody Award, a Gold Medal for Drama from the
National Institute of Arts and Letters, the Literary Lion Award
from the New York Public Library, the John F. Kennedy
Lifetime Achievement Award, and the Algur Meadows Award.
He received honorary degrees from Oxford University and
Harvard University and was awarded the Prix Molière of the
French theatre, the Dorothy and Lillian Gish Lifetime Achieve-
ment Award and the Pulitzer Prize, well as numerous other
awards. He was named the Jefferson Lecturer for the National
Endowment for the Humanities in 2001. He was awarded the
2002 Prince of Asturias Award for Letters and the 2003
Jerusalem Prize.

BY ARTHUR MILLER

DRAMA
The Golden Years
The Man Who Had All the
  Luck
All My Sons
Death of a Salesman
An Enemy of the People
  (*adaptation of the play by Ibsen*)
The Crucible
A View from the Bridge
After the Fall
Incident at Vichy
The Price
The American Clock
The Creation of the World and
  Other Business
The Archbishop's Ceiling
The Ride Down Mt. Morgan
Broken Glass

ONE-ACT PLAYS
A View from the Bridge,
  one-act version, with A Memory
  of Two Mondays
Elegy for a Lady
  (*in* Two-Way Mirror)
Some Kind of Love Story
  (*in* Two-Way Mirror)
I Can't Remember Anything
  (*in* Danger: Memory!)
Clara (*in* Danger: Memory!)
The Last Yankee
Mr. Peters' Connections

OTHER WORKS
Situation Normal
The Misfits (*a cinema novel*)

Focus (*a novel*)
I Don't Need You Anymore
  (*short stories*)
In the Country (*reportage
  with Inge Morath photographs*)
Chinese Encounters (*reportage
  with Inge Morath photographs*)
In Russia (*reportage
  with Inge Morath photographs*)
Salesman in Beijing
  (*a memoir*)
Timebends (*autobiography*)
Homely Girl, A Life
  (*novella*)

COLLECTIONS
Arthur Miller's Collected Plays
  (Volumes I and II)
The Portable Arthur Miller
The Theater Essays of Arthur
  Miller (*Robert Martin, editor*)

VIKING CRITICAL
  LIBRARY EDITIONS
Death of a Salesman
  (*edited by Gerald Weales*)
The Crucible
  (*edited by Gerald Weales*)

TELEVISION WORKS
Playing for Time

SCREENPLAYS
The Misfits
Everybody Wins
The Crucible

THE RIDE DOWN MT. MORGAN

ARTHUR MILLER

PENGUIN BOOKS

PENGUIN BOOKS
Published by the Penguin Group
Penguin Group (USA) Inc., 375 Hudson Street, New York, New York 10014, U.S.A.
Penguin Group (Canada), 10 Alcorn Avenue, Toronto,
Ontario, Canada M4V 3B2 (a division of Pearson Penguin Canada Inc.)
Penguin Books Ltd, 80 Strand, London WC2R 0RL, England
Penguin Ireland, 25 St Stephen's Green, Dublin 2, Ireland (a division of Penguin Books Ltd)
Penguin Group (Australia), 250 Camberwell Road, Camberwell,
Victoria 3124, Australia (a division of Pearson Australia Group Pty Ltd)
Penguin Books India Pvt Ltd, 11 Community Centre,
Panchsheel Park, New Delhi – 110 017, India
Penguin Group (NZ), cnr Airborne and Rosedale Roads,
Albany, Auckland, New Zealand (a division of Pearson New Zealand Ltd)
Penguin Books (South Africa) (Pty) Ltd, 24 Sturdee Avenue,
Rosebank, Johannesburg 2196, South Africa

Penguin Books Ltd, Registered Offices: 80 Strand, London WC2R 0RL, England

First published in Great Britain by Methuen Drama 1991
Published in Penguin Books 1992
This revised edition published in Penguin Books 1999

5 7 9 10 8 6

LIBRARY OF CONGRESS CATALOGING IN PUBLICATION DATA
Miller, Arthur, 1915–
The ride down Mt. Morgan / Arthur Miller.
p.   cm.
ISBN 0 14 04.8244 X
I. Title. II. Title: The ride down Mt. Morgan.
[PS3525.I5156R5   1999]
812'.52—dc21   99-17621

Printed in the United States of America
Set in Bembo
Designed by Ellen Cipriano

TO INGE

PRODUCTION NOTE

The play follows Lyman Felt's mind through scenes in real time as well as in memory and dream. The set must therefore be an open one to allow scenes to move fluidly without pause excepting as noted in the text.

Lyman can leave and enter the hospital bed without having to change in and out of costumes; simply by his drawing covers up near his chin, even though dressed, it is sufficient to suggest him in a hospital gown. Where indicated, however, he should be in a gown.

This final acting version reflects the David Esbjornson production at the Public Theater, New York, in the Fall of 1998.

CAST OF CHARACTERS

LYMAN FELT

THEO FELT

LEAH FELT

BESSIE

NURSE LOGAN

TOM WILSON

THE RIDE DOWN
MT. MORGAN

ACT ONE

SCENE ONE

Lyman Felt asleep in a hospital bed.

Nurse Logan is reading a magazine in a chair a few feet away. She is black. He is deeply asleep, snoring now and then.

LYMAN, *his eyes still shut:* Thank you, thank you all very much. Please be seated. *Nurse turns, looks toward him.* We have a lot of . . . not material . . . yes, material . . . to cover this afternoon, so please take your seats and cross your . . . No-no . . . *Laughs weakly.* . . . Not cross your legs, just take your seats. . . .

NURSE: That was a lot of surgery, Mr. Felt. You're supposed to be resting . . . Or you out?

LYMAN, *for a moment he sleeps, snores, then . . . :* Today I would like you to consider life insurance from a different perspective. I want you to look at the whole economic system as one enormous tit. *Nurse chuckles quietly.* So the job of the individual is to get a good place in line for a suck. *She laughs louder.* Which gives us the word "suckcess." Or . . . or not.

NURSE: You know, you better settle down after all that surgery.

LYMAN, *opens his eyes:* You black?

NURSE: That's what they keep telling me.

LYMAN: Good for you. I've got the biggest training program of any company for you guys. And the first one that ever put them in sales. There's no election now, is there? —Eisenhower or something?

NURSE: It's December. And he's been dead since I don't know when.

LYMAN: Eisenhower *dead? Peers in confusion.* Oh, right, right! . . . Why can't I move, do you mind?

NURSE, *returns to her chair:* You're all in a cast, you broke a lot of bones.

LYMAN: Who?

NURSE: You. You smashed your car. They say you went skiing down that Mount Morgan in a Porsche.

She chuckles. He squints, trying to orient himself.

LYMAN: Where . . . where . . . I'm where?

NURSE: Clearhaven Memorial Hospital.

LYMAN: That Earl Hines?

NURSE: Who?

LYMAN: That piano. Sounds like Earl Hines. *Sings an Earl Hines tune. Laughs appreciatively.* Listen to that, will you? That beautiful? Jimmy Baldwin . . . long, long ago when I was still a writer . . . used to say, "Lyman, you're a nigger underneath." *Chuckles; it fades. Now with some anxiety. . . .* Where?

NURSE: Clearhaven Memorial Hospital.

LYMAN, *it is slowly penetrating: Clearhaven?*

NURSE: Your wife and daughter just arrived up from New York. They're out in the visitors' room.

LYMAN, *canniness attempt, but still confused:* . . . From *New York?* Why? Who called them?

NURSE: What do you mean? Why not?

LYMAN: And where is this?

NURSE: Clearhaven.—I'm from Canada myself, I only just started here. We've still got railroads in Canada.

LYMAN, *a moment of silent confusion:* Listen. I'm not feeling well . . . why are we talking about Canadian railroads?

NURSE: No, I just mentioned it, as there is a storm.

LYMAN: Now what . . . what . . . what was that about my wife . . . New York?

NURSE: She's here in the waiting room . . .

LYMAN: Here in the waiting . . .

NURSE: . . . And your daughter.

LYMAN, *tension rising with clearing of mind; he looks at his hands, turns them over:* . . . Would you mind?—Just . . . touch me? *She touches his face; he angers with the fully dawning fact.* Who the hell called them, for God's sake? Why didn't somebody ask me?

NURSE: I'm new here! I'm sorry if I'm not satisfactory.

LYMAN, *high anxiety:* Who said you're not satisfactory? What is this . . . endless . . . *verbiage?*—not verbiage, for Christ's sake, I meant . . . *Panting.* Listen, I absolutely can't see anyone and they have to go back to New York right away.

NURSE: But as long as you're awake . . .

LYMAN: Immediately! Go—get them out of here! *A jab of pain.* Ow!—Please, quickly, go!—Wait!—There's no . . . like another . . . you know, woman out there?

NURSE: Not while I was out there.

LYMAN: Please . . . quickly, huh? I can't see anybody. *Bewildered, Nurse exits.* Oh, poor Theo—here! My God, what have

I done! How could I have gone out on that road in a storm! *Terrified of self-betrayal.* Have you lost your fucking mind?! *Frozen in anguish, he stares straight ahead as music is heard. His mood changes as he is caught by his catastrophic vision.* Oh, dear God, this mustn't happen.

His wife, Theo, and daughter, Bessie, are discovered seated on a waiting room settee. A burst of weeping from Bessie. He is not looking directly at them but imagining them.

Oh, Bessie, my poor Bessie! *Covers his eyes, as Bessie weeps.* No-no-no, it mustn't happen!—think of something else!—

His vision is forcing him out of the bed in his hospital gown. Music fades out.

THEO, *touching Bessie's hand:* Darling, try not to.

BESSIE: I can't help it.

THEO: Of course you can. Be brave now, dear.

LYMAN, *moving into the range of the women:* Oh yes! My Theo! That's exactly what she'd say! What a woman!

THEO: Try to think of all the happiness; think of his laughter; Daddy loves life, he'll fight for it.

BESSIE: . . . I guess I've just never had anything really bad happen.

LYMAN, *a few feet away:* Oh, my dear child . . . !

THEO: But you'll see as you get older—everything ultimately fits together . . . and for the good.

LYMAN, *staring front:* Oh yes . . . good old Episcopal Theo!

THEO: —Now come, Bessie.—Remember what a wonderful time we had in Africa? Think of Africa.

BESSIE: What an amazing woman you are, Mother.

Nurse Logan enters.

NURSE: It'll still be a while before he can see anybody.
Would you like me to call a motel? It's ski season, but my
husband can probably get you in, he plows their driveway.

BESSIE: Do you know if he's out of danger?

NURSE: I'm sure the doctors will let you know. *Obviously
changing the subject.* I can't believe you made it up from New
York in this sleet.

THEO: One does what one has to. Actually . . . would you
mind calling the motel? It was a terrible drive . . .

NURSE: Sometimes I feel like going back to Canada—at
least we had a railroad.

THEO: We'll have them again; things take time in this country but in the end we get them done.

NURSE: Don't hesitate if you want more tea.

Nurse exits.

THEO, *turns to Bessie, smiling painfully:* Why'd you start to laugh?

BESSIE, *touching Theo's hand:* It's nothing . . .

THEO: Well, what is it?

BESSIE: Well . . . I mean things really don't always get done in this country.

THEO, *disengaging her hand; she is hurt:* I think they do, ultimately. I've lived through changes that were inconceivable thirty years ago. *Straining to laugh.* Really, dear, I'm not *that* naive.

BESSIE, *angering:* Well, don't be upset!—They certainly are very nice people around here, aren't they?

THEO, *managing to pull her mood together:* I'm sorry you never knew small town life—there is a goodness.

BESSIE: I'm wondering if we should call Grandma Esther.

THEO, *dutifully:* If you like. *Slight pause. Bessie is still.* She gets so impressively emotional, that's all. But call . . . she *is* his mother.

BESSIE: I know she's a superficial woman, but I can't help it, I . . .

THEO: But you *should* like her, she adores you; she simply never liked me and I've always known it, that's all. *She looks away.*

BESSIE: I mean she can be awfully funny sometimes. And she *is* warm.

THEO: Warm? Yes, I suppose—provided it doesn't commit her to anything or anyone. I've never hidden it, dear—I think she's the center of his psychological problem . . .

LYMAN: Perfect!

THEO: . . . But I suppose I'm prejudiced.

Lyman laughs silently with a head shake of joyful recognition.

I used to think it was because he didn't marry Jewish, but . . .

BESSIE: But she didn't either.

THEO: Darling, she'd have disliked any woman he married . . . except an heiress or a sexpot. But go ahead, I do think you should call her. *Bessie stands.* And give her my love, will you?

Lyman issues a cackling laugh of appreciation of her nature.

Leah enters. She is in her thirties; in an open raccoon coat, high heels. Nurse enters with her.

LYMAN, *on the instant she enters, claps his hands over his eyes:* No, she mustn't! It can't happen! She mustn't! *Unable to bear it, he starts to flee, but stops as . . .*

LEAH: After all the money we've put into this hospital it seems to me I ought to be able to speak to the chief nurse, for Christ's sake!

NURSE: I'm doing my best to get her for you . . . !

LEAH: Well hurry, will you? *Nurse starts to exit.* I'm only asking for a little information, dear!

Nurse exits. Pause.

LYMAN, *imploring himself, his eyes clamped shut:* Think of something else. Let's see now—the new Mercedes convertible . . . that actress, what's her name . . . ? *But he fails to escape; and scared, slowly turns his head toward . . .*

Leah, who sits, but quickly stands again and moves restlessly. Theo and Bessie observe her indirectly, with polite curiosity. Now their eyes meet. Leah throws up her hands.

LEAH: The same thing when I had my baby here, it was like pulling teeth to get them to tell me if it was a boy or a girl.

BESSIE: Is it an emergency?

LEAH: Yes, my husband; he cracked up the car on Mount Morgan. You?

BESSIE: My father. It was a car, too.

LYMAN, *eyes heavenward, hands clasped:* Oh please, please!

THEO: The roads are impossible.

LEAH: I can't imagine what got into him, driving down Mount Morgan on ice . . . and at night yet! It's incomprehensible! *A sudden explosion.* Damn them, I have a right to know what's happening! *She charges out.*

BESSIE: Poor thing.

THEO: But she *knows* how busy they are . . .

Silence now; Theo leans back, closing her eyes. Another sobbing fit threatens Bessie, who downs it, covers her eyes. Then suddenly she breaks down and weeps.

Oh Bessie, dear, try not to.

BESSIE, *shaking her head helplessly:* . . . I just love him so!

Leah returns, more subdued now. She sits tiredly, closes her eyes. Pause. She gets up, goes to a window, looks out.

LEAH: *Now* the moon comes out!—everybody smashes up in the dark and now you could read a paper out there.

BESSIE: You live around here?

LEAH: Not far. We're out near the lake.

BESSIE: It looks like beautiful country.

LEAH: Oh, it is. But I'll take New York anytime. *A great sob suddenly bursts from her; she chokes it back.* I'm sorry. *But she weeps again, helplessly into her handkerchief. Bessie is affected and begins weeping, too.*

THEO: Now really . . . ! *Shakes Bessie's arm.* Stop this! *She sees Leah's indignant look.* You still don't know how serious it is, why do you carry on like this?

LEAH, *rather unwillingly:* You're probably right.

THEO, *exulting—to Bessie as well:* Of course! I mean there's always time to despair, why should . . . ?

LEAH, *sharply:* I *said* you were right, I was agreeing with you! *Theo turns away stiffly.* I'm sorry.

Now the women go motionless.

LYMAN, *marveling:* What strong, admirable women they are! What definite characters! Thank God I'm only imagining this to torture myself . . . But it's enough! *Starts resolutely toward the bed, but caught by his vision, halts.* Now what would they say next?

The women reanimate.

BESSIE: You raise things on your place?

LEAH: We grow most of what we eat. And we're starting to raise a few thoroughbreds now, in a small way.

BESSIE: Oh, I'd love that . . .

LEAH: I envy your composure—both of you. Really, you make me feel better. What part of New York are you in?

BESSIE: East Seventy-fourth Street.

LYMAN: Oh no! No no!

LEAH: Really! We often stay at the Carlyle . . .

BESSIE: Oh, it's practically around the corner.

THEO: You sound like a New Yorker.

LEAH: I went to NYU School of Business for three years; I loved it but I was raised up here in Elmira . . . and my business is here, so . . .

THEO: What sort of business do you have?

LEAH: Insurance.

BESSIE: That's what Daddy does!

LYMAN, *knocking his knuckles against his head:* No-no-no-no-no!

LEAH: Well, there's a million of us. You in it too?

BESSIE: No, I'm at home . . . take care of my husband.

LEAH: I'm hoping to sell out in a couple of years, get a place in Manhattan somewhere, and just paint morning to night the rest of my life.

BESSIE: Really! My husband's a painter.

LEAH: Professionally, or . . . ?

BESSIE: Oh yes. He's Harold Lamb.

Lyman rushes over to the bed and pulls the covers over his head.

LEAH: Harold Lamb?

Leah ceases all movement, staring at Bessie. She turns to stare at Theo.

THEO: What is it?

LEAH: Your husband is really Harold Lamb?

BESSIE, *very pleased and proud:* You've heard of him?

LEAH: You're not Mrs. Felt, are you?

THEO: Why yes.

LEAH, *her puzzled look:* Then you . . . *Breaks off, then . . .* You're not here for Lyman, are you?

BESSIE: You know Daddy?

LEAH: But . . . *Turning from one to the other* . . . how'd they come to notify *you?*

LYMAN, *sits up in bed and raises a devout, monitory hand to heaven, whispering loudly:* Stop it, stop it, stop it . . . !

THEO, *uncomprehending, but beginning to take affront:* Why shouldn't they notify me?

LEAH: Well . . . after so many years.

THEO: What do you mean?

LEAH: But it's over nine . . .

THEO: What is?

LEAH: Your divorce.

Theo and Bessie are struck dumb. A silence.

You're Theodora Felt, right?

THEO: Who *are* you?

LEAH: I'm Leah. Leah Felt.

THEO, *a haughtiness begins:* Felt!

LEAH: Lyman is my husband.

THEO: Who *are* you? What are you talking about!

BESSIE, *intensely curious about Leah, she angers at Theo:* Well don't get *angry,* for heaven's sake!

THEO: Be quiet!

LEAH, *seeing Theo's genuineness:* Well, you're divorced, aren't you?

THEO: Divorced!—who the hell *are* you!

LEAH: I'm Lyman's wife. *Theo sees she is a serious woman; it silences her.*

BESSIE: When . . . when did you . . . ? I mean . . .

THEO, *in motion again:* She's insane!—she's some kind of a nut!

LEAH, *to Bessie:* It was nine years this past July.

THEO: Really. And who performed this . . . this *event?*

LEAH: The Reno City Hall clerk, later a rabbi here in Elmira. My son's name is Benjamin, for Lyman's father, and Alexander for his great-grandmother—Benjamin Alexander Felt.

THEO, *with a weak attempt to sustain mockery:* Really!

LEAH: Yes, I'm terribly sorry if you didn't know.

THEO: Didn't know *what?* What are you *talking* about?

LEAH: We have been married a little over nine years, Mrs. Felt.

THEO: Have you? And I suppose you have some document . . . ?

LEAH: I have our marriage certificate, I guess . . .

THEO: You guess!

LEAH, *angrily:* Well I'm sure I do! And I know I have Lyman's will in our safe deposit box . . .

THEO, *helplessly mocking:* And it names you as his wife!

LEAH: And Benjamin as his son. *Theo is halted by her factuality. . . .* But I guess you have more or less the same . . . is that right? *Theo is still as a stone.* There really was no divorce?

BESSIE, *with a glance at her stricken mother . . . softly, almost apologetically:* . . . No.

LEAH: Well, I guess we'd better . . . meet, or something. And talk. *Theo is staring into space.* Mrs. Felt? I understand your feelings, but you'll just have to believe it, I guess—we have a terrible problem. Mrs. Felt?

THEO: It's impossible, nine years ago . . . *To Bessie:* That's when we all went to Africa.

BESSIE: Oh, right!—the safari!

THEO, *to Leah, with a victorious, if nearly demented laugh:* We were never closer in our lives! We traveled through Kenya, Nigeria . . . *As though this clinched everything.* . . . we even flew to Egypt!

Nurse enters. It instantly galvanizes all of them. She glances from one to the other.

NURSE: Doctor Lowry would like to see Mrs. Felt now.

For one instant no one moves—then both Theo and Leah rise simultaneously. This actualization of Leah's claim stiffens Theo, forcing her to start assertively toward the Nurse—and she sways and starts to fall to the floor.

LEAH: Catch her!

BESSIE: Mother!

Nurse and Bessie catch Theo, then lower her to the floor.

LEAH, *over her shoulder:* Help here, someone's fainted! Where the hell is a doctor, goddammit! *To the air:* Is there a doctor in this fucking hospital?!

BLACKOUT.

SCENE TWO

A couch and chair. Leah is seated facing Tom Wilson, a middle-aged but very fit lawyer who is reading a will, and sipping coffee. After a moment she gets up and moves to a point and stares, eyes filled with fear. Then dialing a cell phone, turns to him.

LEAH: Sure you wouldn't like some toast?—Sorry I'm not being much of a hostess.

TOM, *immersed:* Thanks. I'm just about done here.

LEAH, *dialing:* God, I dread it—my boy'll be home any minute . . . *Into phone:* Put my brother on, Tina. . . . Lou?— I don't know, they won't let me see him yet. What'd Uniroyal say? *What?* Well get on it, will you, call L.A. this minute! I mean for God's sake, Lou, I want that business! *Hangs up.* How much do you have to pay relatives to get them to do any work? *Tom closes the file, turns to her, silent.* —I know you're her lawyer, but I'm not really asking advice, am I?

TOM: I can discuss this. *Returns her file.* The will does recognize the boy as his son, but you are not his wife.

LEAH, *lifting the file:* Even if this refers to me as his wife?

TOM: I'm afraid that's legally meaningless, since he never divorced. However . . . *Breaks off, pressing his eyes.* I'm just stunned, I simply can't absorb it.

LEAH: I'm still in midair someplace.

TOM: What'd you ask me? Oh yes—provided the legal wife gets a minimum of one third of the estate he can leave you as much as he likes. So you're very well taken care of. *Sighs, leaning forward and gripping his head.* He actually flies a plane, you say?

LEAH: Oh yes, soaring planes, too.

TOM: You know, for years he'd never get off the ground unless it was unavoidable.

LEAH: Oh, he's wonderful in the air. *Pause.* I'm not here. I'm simply . . . not here. Can he be two people? Is that possible?

TOM: . . . May I ask you . . . ?

LEAH: Please. . . . Incidentally, have you known him long?

TOM: Sixteen, seventeen years.—When you decided to marry, I assume he told you he'd gotten a divorce . . .

LEAH: Of course. We went to Reno together.

TOM: No kidding! And what happened?

LEAH: God, I'd forgotten all about this . . . *Breaks off.* How could I be so *stupid!* —You see, it was July, streets were boiling hot, so he had me stay in the hotel while he went to pick up his divorce decree . . . *She goes silent.*

TOM: Yes?

LEAH, *shaking her head:* God!—my gullibility!—I was curious to see what a decree looked like, so . . .

Lyman enters, wearing a short-sleeved summer shirt and cowboy hat.

No particular reason, but I'd never seen one . . .

LYMAN: I threw it away.

LEAH, *with a surprised laugh:* Why!

LYMAN: I don't want to look back, I feel twenty-five! *Laughs.* You look stunned!

LEAH: I guess I never believed you'd marry me, darling.

LYMAN, *he draws her to him:* Feeling is all I really believe in, Leah—you're making me see that again. Feeling is chaos, but any decent thing I've ever done was out of feeling, and every lousy thing I'm ashamed of came from careful thinking. I simply can't lose you, Leah, you're precious to me. —You look scared . . . what is it?

LEAH: I don't want to say it.

LYMAN: Go ahead. Please!

LEAH: Every relationship I've known gets to where it needs a lie to keep it going.

LYMAN: But does that always have to be!

LEAH, *hesitates:* Can I say something? I wish we could make a different wedding vow; like "Dearly beloved, I promise everything good, but I might have to lie to you sometimes." *He is taken aback, but grins.* —I wanted to say that, okay? You're shocked, aren't you.

LYMAN: What balls you have to say that! —Come here. *Takes her hand, closes his eyes.* I'm going to learn to fly a plane.

LEAH: What are you talking about?

LYMAN: Because flying terrifies me. I'm going to wrestle down one fear at a time till I've dumped them all and I am a free man! *Gripping her hands, nose to nose.* I have a car and driver downstairs. *Holds out his beckoning arm.* Come to your wedding, Leah, my darling!

Lyman exits without lowering his arm.

LEAH: . . . And it was all lies! How is it possible! Why did he do it? What did he want?

TOM: Actually, though . . . *Tries to recall.* Yes, I think it was about nine years ago, we did have a discussion about a divorce . . . although at the time I didn't take it all that seriously. He suddenly popped in one day with this "research" he said he'd done . . .

Lyman enters in a business suit. Tom has moved out of Leah's area.

LYMAN: . . . I've been looking into bigamy, Tom.

TOM, *laughs, surprised:* Bigamy!—what are you talking about?

LYMAN: You know there's an enormous amount of it in the United States now.

TOM: Really? But what's the point . . . ?

LYMAN: . . . And not just among blacks or the poor. I've been wondering about a desertion insurance policy. Might call it the Bigamy Protection Plan. *Tom laughs.* I'm serious. We could set the premiums really low. Be great, especially for minority women.

TOM, *admiringly:* Say now! Where the hell do you get these ideas?

LYMAN: Just put myself in other people's places. —Incidentally, how frequently do they prosecute for bigamy anymore, you have any idea?

TOM: None whatsoever. But it's a victimless crime so it can't be often.

LYMAN: That's my impression, too. Get somebody to research it, will you, I want to be sure. —I'll be in Elmira till Friday. *Lyman starts to leave but dawdles.*

TOM: Why do I think you're depressed?

LYMAN: . . . I guess I am—slightly. *The grin.* I'm turning fifty-four this July.

TOM: Fifty's much tougher, I think.

LYMAN: My father died at fifty-three.

TOM: Well, you're over the hump. Anyway, you're in better shape than anybody I know.

LYMAN: Famous last words.

TOM: Something wrong, Lyman?

LYMAN: I don't think I have the balls. *A laugh. Moves into high tension; then, facing his challenge, turns rather abruptly to Tom.* There's no man I trust like you, Tom. *A grin.* —I guess you know I've cheated on Theodora.

TOM: Well, I've had my suspicions, yes—ever since I walked in on you humping that Pakistani typist on your desk.

LYMAN, *laughs:* "Humping!" —I love that Presbyterian jive of yours, haven't heard that in years.

TOM: Quaker.

LYMAN, *confessionally, quietly:* There've been more than that one, Tommy.

TOM, *laughs:* God, where do you get the time?

LYMAN: Disgust you?

TOM: Not catastrophically.

LYMAN, *pause; he composes himself, then . . . again with the grin:*
I think I've fallen in love.

TOM: Oh Lyman . . . don't tell me!

LYMAN, *pointing at him and laughing nervously:* Look at you!—
God, you really love Theodora, don't you!

TOM: Of course I do!—you're not thinking of divorce,
are you?

LYMAN: I don't know. Maybe I just wanted to say it aloud to
somebody.

TOM: But how sure are you about your feelings for this
woman?

LYMAN: I'm sure. A new woman has always been an undis-
covered shore, but I'd really like to go straight now, Tom. I
want one woman for the rest of my life. And I can't quite see
it being Theodora.

TOM: You know she loves you deeply, Lyman.

LYMAN: Tom, I love her, too. But after thirty-two years we
bore each other, we just do. And boredom is a form of deception, isn't it. And deception has become like my Nazi, my
worst horror—I want nothing now but to wear my own face
on my face every day till the day I die. Or do you think that
kind of honesty is possible?

TOM: I don't have to tell you, the problem is not honesty
but how much you hurt others with it.

LYMAN: Right. What about your religion? But there's no solution there either, I guess.

TOM: I somehow can't imagine you praying, Lyman. *Short pause.*

LYMAN: Is there an answer?

TOM: I don't know, maybe all one can do is hope to end up with the right regrets.

LYMAN: You ever cheated, Tom?

TOM: No.

LYMAN: Honest to God?—I've seen you eye the girls around here.

TOM: It's the truth.

LYMAN: Is that the regret you end up with?

Tom laughs bashfully, then Lyman joins him. And suddenly, Lyman's embarrassment and suffering are on his face.

. . . Shit, that was cruel, Tom, forgive me, will you? Dammit, why do I let myself get depressed? It's all pointless guilt, that's all! Here I start from nothing, create forty-two hundred jobs for people and raise over sixty ghetto blacks to office positions when that was not easy to do—I should be proud of myself, son of a bitch! And I am! I am! *He bangs on the desk, then subsides, looks front and downward.* I love your view. That red river of taillights gliding down Park Avenue on a winter's night—and all those silky white thighs crossing inside those heated limousines . . . Christ, can there be a sexier vision in the world? *Turning back to Tom.* I keep thinking of my father—how connected he was to his life; couldn't wait to open the store every morning and happily count the pickles, rearrange the olive barrels. People like that knew the main thing. Which is what? What is the main thing, do you know?

Tom is silent.

—Look, don't worry, I really can't imagine myself without Theodora, she's a great, great wife! . . . I love that woman! It's always good talking to you, Tom. *Starts to go, halts.* Maybe it's simply that if you try to live according to your real desires, you have to end up looking like a shit.

Lyman exits. Leah covers her face and there is a pause as Tom observes her.

TOM: I'm sorry.

LEAH: He had it all carefully worked out from the very beginning.

TOM: I'd say it was more like . . . a continuous improvisation.

LEAH: It was the baby, you see—once I was pregnant he simply wouldn't listen to reason . . .

Lyman hurries on in a winter overcoat, claps a hand over her mouth.

LYMAN: Don't tell me it's too late. *Kisses her.* Did you do it?

LEAH: I was just walking out the door for the hospital.

LYMAN: Oh, thank God. *Draws her to a seat, and pulls her down.* Please, dear, give me one full minute and then you can do as you like.

LEAH, *with pain:* Don't, Lyme, it's impossible.

LYMAN: You know if you do this it's going to change it between us.

LEAH: Darling, it comes down to being a single parent and I just don't want that.

LYMAN: I've already named him.

LEAH, *amused, touching his face:* How do you know it's a him?

LYMAN: I'm never wrong. I have a very intimate relationship with ladies' bellies. His name is Benjamin after my father and Alexander after my mother's mother, who I loved a lot. *Grins at his own egoism.* You can put in a middle name.

LEAH, *with an unhappy laugh:* Well thanks so much! *She tries to stand up but he holds her.* He asked me not to be late.

LYMAN: The Russians—this is an ancient custom—before an important parting, they sit for a moment in silence. Give Benjamin this moment.

LEAH: He's not Benjamin, now stop it!

LYMAN: Believe in your feelings, Leah, the rest is nonsense. What do you really and truly want?

Silence for a moment.

I would drive him to school in the mornings and take him to ball games.

LEAH: Twice a month?

LYMAN: With the new office set up here, I could easily be with you more than half the time.

LEAH: And Theodora?

LYMAN: It's difficult to talk about her.

LEAH: With me, you mean?

LYMAN: I can't lie to myself, darling, she's been a tremendous wife. It would be too unjust.

LEAH: But keeping it a secret—where does that leave me? It's hard enough to identify myself as it is. And I can't believe she won't find out sooner or later, and then what?

LYMAN: If I actually have to choose it'll be you. But she doesn't know a soul in this whole area, it'd be a million-to-one shot for her to ever find out. I'm practically with you half the time now, and it's been pretty good, hasn't it?

LEAH, *touching her belly:* . . . But what do we tell this? . . .

LYMAN: . . . Benjamin.

LEAH: Oh stop calling him Benjamin! It's not even three weeks!

LYMAN: That's long enough to be Benjamin—he has a horoscope, stars and planets; he has a *future!*

LEAH: . . . Why do I feel we're circling around something? There's something I don't believe here—what is it?

LYMAN: Maybe that I'm this desperate. *Kisses her belly.*

LEAH: Are you? —I can't express it . . . there's just something about this baby that doesn't seem . . . I don't know—inevitable.

LYMAN: Darling, I haven't wanted anything this much since my twenties, when I was struggling to be a poet and make something of my own that would last.

LEAH: Really.

LYMAN: It's the truth.

LEAH: That's touching, Lyman, I'm very moved.

So it is up in the air for a moment.

But I can't, I won't, it's the story of my life, I always end up with all the responsibility; I'd have to be in total charge of your child and I know I'd resent it finally—and maybe even you as well. You're putting me back to being twelve or thirteen and my parents asking *me* where to go on vacation, or what kind of car to buy or what color drapes. I hate that position! One of the most sensuous things about you was that I could lie back and let you drive, and now you're putting me behind the wheel again. It's just all wrong.

LYMAN: I thought if we lived together let's say ten years, you'd still be in the prime, and pretty rich, and I'd . . .

LEAH: . . . Walk away into the sunset.

LYMAN: I'm trying to be as cruelly realistic as life, darling. Have you ever loved a man the way you love me?

LEAH: No.

LYMAN: Well? That's the only reality.

LEAH: You can drive me to the hospital, if you like realism so much. *She stands; he does.* You look so sad! You poor man.

She kisses him; a silent farewell is in the kiss; she gets her coat and turns to him.

I won't weaken on this, dear, so make up your mind.

LYMAN: We're going to lose each other if you do this. I feel it.

LEAH: Well, there's a very simple way not to lose me, dear, I guess that's why they invented it. —Come, wait in the hospital if you want to. If not, I'll be back tomorrow. *She draws him on, but he halts.*

LYMAN: Will you give me a week to tell her? It's still early for you, isn't it?

LEAH: Tell her what?

LYMAN: . . . That I'm going to marry you.

TOM: I see.

Lyman moves into darkness.

LEAH: I don't understand it; he'd had dozens of women, why did he pick me to be irreplaceable? *She looks down at her watch, stares in silence.* God! How do I tell my boy?

TOM: He's nine now?

LEAH: And worships Lyman. Worships him.

TOM: I'd better get to the hospital. *He moves to go, halts hesitantly.* Don't answer this if you'd rather not, but you think you could ever take him back?

LEAH, *thinks for a moment:* How could you ask me that? It's outrageous! —Would Theodora? She struck me as a rather judgmental sort of woman.

TOM: Oh, she has a tender side, too. —I guess she hasn't had time to think of the future, any more than you have.

LEAH: All this reminds me of an idea I used to have about him that . . . well, it'll sound mystical and silly . . .

TOM: Please. I'd love to understand him.

LEAH: Well, it's just that he wants so much; like a kid at a fair; a jelly apple here, a cotton candy there, and then a ride on a loop-the-loop . . . and it never lets up in him; it's what's so attractive about him—to women, I mean—Lyman's mind is up your skirt but it's such a rare thing to be wanted like that—indifference is what most men feel now—I mean they have an appetite but not hunger—and here is such a splendidly hungry man and it's simply . . . well . . . precious once you're past twenty-five. I tell you the truth, somewhere deep down I think I sensed something about him wasn't on the level, but . . . I guess I must have loved him so much that I . . . *Breaks off.* —But I mustn't talk this way; he's unforgivable! It's the rottenest thing I've ever heard of! The answer is no, absolutely not!

TOM, *nods, thinks, then . . . :* Well, I'll be off. I hope it's not too difficult for you with the little boy. *He exits.*

Blackout on Leah.

SCENE THREE

Lyman is softly snoring; a deep troubled sleep, however; bad dreams, muttering, an arm raised in a gesture.

Tom enters with Nurse. She raises Lyman's eyelid.

NURSE: He still goes in and out but you can try him.

TOM: Lyman? Can you hear me? *Lyman stops snoring but eyes remain shut.* It's Tom Wilson.

NURSE: Keep going, he shouldn't be staying under this much by now.

TOM: Lyman, it's Tom.

LYMAN, *opens his eyes:* You in the store?

TOM: It's the hospital.

LYMAN: Hospital? Oh right, right . . . Jesus, I was dreaming of my father's store; every time he looked at me he'd shake his head and say, "Hopeless case." *Laughs tiredly, trying to focus.* Give me a second; little mixed up. How'd you get here?

TOM: Theodora called me.

LYMAN: Theodora?

TOM: Your car is registered in the city so the state police called her.

LYMAN: I had some weird dream that she and Bessie . . . *Breaks off.* They're not here, are they?

NURSE: I told you your wife came . . .

TOM, *to Nurse:* Excuse us, please?

NURSE: But I told him. *She exits.*

TOM: They've met, Lyman.

LYMAN, *pause; he struggles to orient himself:* Theo . . . didn't collapse, did she?

TOM: Yes, but she's come around, she'll be all right.

LYMAN: I don't understand it, I think I dreamed the whole thing . . .

TOM: Well, that wouldn't be too difficult, it's all pretty inevitable.

LYMAN: Why're you being so brutal?

TOM: There's no time to fool around, you've got things to decide. It's all over television . . .

LYMAN: Oh. —Have you met her?—Leah? I'm finished.

TOM: We've had a talk. She's a considerable woman.

LYMAN, *gratefully:* Isn't she? —She's furious, too, huh?

TOM: Well, what do you expect?

LYMAN: See . . . I thought I'd somehow divorce Theo later. —But it sort of settled in where I had both of them. And after a while it didn't seem so godawful . . . . What about Bessie?

TOM: It's hit her pretty bad, I guess.

LYMAN: God, and poor little Benny! Jesus, if I could go through the ceiling and just disappear.

TOM: The television is flogging it. I think you ought to issue a press statement to cut the whole thing short. As to your intentions.

LYMAN: What intentions? Just give each of them whatever they want. I'll probably go and live somewhere . . . maybe like Brazil or something . . .

TOM: You won't try to hold on to either of them.

LYMAN: Are you mad? They wouldn't have anything to do with me. My God . . . *He turns away, tears in his eyes.* How could I have destroyed everything like this!—my character! *Higher intensity:* Why did I drive into that storm?—I can't understand it! I had the room in the Howard Johnson's, I think I was even in bed . . . figured I'd wait out the storm there . . . Why'd I go out into it again?

TOM: Can you give Theo a few minutes? She wants to say good-bye.

LYMAN: How can I face her? Ask her to wait till tomorrow, maybe I'll feel a little better and . . .

Theo and Bessie enter; Lyman does not see them, as they are above him.

TOM: They're here, Lyman.

Lyman closes his eyes, breathing fast. Bessie, holding Theo by the elbow, accompanies her to the bedside.

BESSIE, *whispering with some shock:* Look at his bandages! *Turning away.* Oh, Mother!

THEO: Stop that. *Bending to Lyman:* Lyman? *He can't get himself to speak.* It's Theodora.

LYMAN, *opening his eyes:* Hi.

THEO: How are you feeling?

LYMAN: Not too bad now. I hope I make sense with all this painkiller . . . Is that you, Bessie?

BESSIE: I'm only here because of Mother.

LYMAN: Oh. Okay. I'm sorry, Bess—I mean that my character's so bad. But I'm proud that you have enough strength to despise me.

BESSIE: But who wouldn't?

LYMAN: Good! *His voice starts to break but he controls himself.* That was well-spoken, sweetie.

BESSIE, *with quick anger:* Don't call me that . . .

THEO, *to Bessie:* Shhh! *She has been observing him in silence.* Lyman? —Is it true?

Lyman closes his eyes.

I have to hear it from you. Did you marry that woman?

Deep snores.

More urgently: Lyman?

BESSIE, *points:* He's not really sleeping!

THEO: Did you have a child with that woman? Lyman? I insist!!! I insist!!!

Lyman emerges from the upstage side of the bed, hands clapped to his ears, while Theo and Bessie continue addressing the bed, as though he were still in it.

Light change: an ethereal colorlessness now, air devoid of pigment.

LYMAN, *agonized cry, ears still covered:* I hear you!

Theo continues to address the bed, and Bessie is fixed on it as well, but their attitude becomes formalized as they become part of his vision.

THEO: What in God's name have you done!

Almost writhing in conflict, Lyman clears his throat. He remains a distance upstage of the bed.

BESSIE, *bent over the bed:* Shh! He's saying something!

LYMAN: I realize . . . how crazy it sounds, Theodora . . . *Breaks off.*

THEO: Yes?

LYMAN: . . . I'm not really sure, but . . . I wonder if this crash . . . was maybe to sort of subconsciously . . . get you both to . . . meet one another, finally.

THEO, *with disgust:* Meet *her?*

LYMAN: I know it sounds absurd but . . .

THEO: Absurd! —It's disgusting! She's exactly the type who forgets to wash out her panties.

LYMAN, *wincing, but with a certain pleasurable recognition:* I *knew* you'd say that! —I admit it, though, there is a sloppy side to her . . .

THEO: She's the worst generation in our history—screw anybody in pants, then drop their litters like cats, and spout mystic credos on cosmic responsibility, ecology, and human rights!

LYMAN: To my dying day I will stand amazed at your ability to speak in complete paragraphs!

THEO: I insist you explain this to me yourself. Lyman? Lyman!

Leah enters. Theo reacts instantly.

There'll be no one in here but family! *To Bessie:* Get the nurse!

LEAH, *despite Theo, approaches the cast, but with uncertainty about his reaction to her:* Lyman?

THEO, *to Tom:* Get her out of here! *Tom is immobile, and she goes to him furiously.* She does not belong here!

LEAH, *to the cast, with a certain warmth:* It's me, Lyme. Can you hear me?

THEO, *rushing threateningly toward Leah:* Get out, get out, get out . . . !

Just as she is about to lay hands on Leah, Lyman throws his arms up and cries imploringly.

LYMAN: I want everybody to lie down!

The three women instantly deanimate as though suddenly falling under the urgency of his control. Lyman gestures, without actually touching them, and causes Theo and Leah to lie on the bed.

LEAH, *as she lies down; voice soft, remote:* What am I going to tell Benny? Oh gee whiz, Lyman, why did you . . . ?

THEO, *lying down beside Leah:* You have a bitter smell, you should use something.

LEAH: I have, but he likes it.

THEO: Blah. *To Lyman:* And what would you say if one of us took another man to bed and asked you to lie next to him?

LYMAN, *lifting off her glasses:* Oh, I'd kill him, dear; but you're a lady, Theodora; the delicate sculpture of your noble eye, your girlish faith in me and your disillusion; your idealism and your unadmitted greed for wealth; the awkward tenderness of your wooden fingers, your incurably Protestant cooking; your savoir-faire and your sexual inexperience; your sensible shoes and devoted motherhood, your intolerant former radicalism and stalwart love of country now—your Theodorism! Who can ever take your place!

LEAH, *laughing:* Why am I laughing!!

LYMAN: Because you're an anarchist, my darling! *He stretches out on both of them.* Oh, what pleasure, what intensity! Your countercurrents are like bare live wires! *Kisses each in turn.* I'd have no problem defending both of you to the death! Oh the double heat of two blessed wives—this is heaven! *Rests his head on Leah while holding Theo's hand to his cheek.*

LEAH: Listen, you've got to make up your mind about something.

LYMAN: I'm only delaying as long as possible, let's delay it till we all die! Delay, delay, how delicious, my loving Leah, is delay!

THEO, *sits up:* How you can still go on talking about love is beyond my understanding.

LYMAN: And still I love you, Theodora, although certain parts of your body fill me with *rage!*

THEO: So you simply got yourself some other parts instead.

Leah, still lying on her back, raises one leg in the air, and her skirt slides down, exposing her thigh.

LYMAN, *replying to Theo, kissing Leah's thigh:* That's the truth, yes—at least it was all flesh at first.

LEAH, *stretching out her arms and her body:* Oh, how good that was! I'm still pulsing to the tips of my toes. *Theo helps him into shirt and trousers and hands him a jacket.*

You're really healthy, aren't you.

LYMAN, *they are moving out of Theo's area:* You mean for my age? Yes.

LEAH: I did not mean that!

Loud knocking heard. She turns upstage with slight shock. A man's angry voice, muffled words. She stands motionless.

LYMAN: You okay?

LEAH: It's nothing! Do you have time for a walk?

LYMAN: My health is terrific; in fact, it keeps threatening my dignity.

A park bench appears.

LEAH: Why!

LYMAN: Well, how do I come to be lounging in a park with a girl, and on a working day! I really hadn't planned to do that this afternoon. Did you know I was going to?

LEAH: No . . . but I never do.

LYMAN: Really? But you seem so organized.

LEAH: In business; but not in pleasure.

LYMAN: What surprised me was the openness of your laughter with those heavy executives at the table.

LEAH: Well, your presentation was so funny, I'd heard you were a real brain, not a comic.

LYMAN: Well, insurance is basically comical, isn't it?—at least pathetic.

LEAH: Why?

LYMAN: You're buying immortality, aren't you?—reaching out of your grave to pay the bills and remind people of your life? It's poetry. The soul was once immortal, now we've got an insurance policy.

LEAH: You sound pretty cynical about it.

LYMAN: Not at all—I started as a writer, nobody lusts after the immortal like a writer.

LEAH: How'd you get into insurance?

LYMAN: Pure accident. How'd you?

LEAH: My mother had died, my dad had his stroke, and insurance was something I could do from home. Dad knew a lot of people, being a doctor, so the thing just took off.

LYMAN: Don't take this wrong—but you know what I find terrifically sexy about you?

LEAH: What?

LYMAN: Your financial independence. Horrible, huh?

LEAH: Why?—*wryly*—Whatever helps, helps.

LYMAN: You don't sound married, are you?

LEAH: It's a hell of a time to ask! *They laugh, come closer.* I can't see myself getting married . . . not yet anyway. —Incidentally, have you been listening to me?

LYMAN: Yes, but my attention keeps wandering toward a warm and furry place . . . *She laughs, delighted.* It's funny, my generation got married to show its maturity, yours stays single for the same reason.

LEAH: That's good!

LYMAN: How happy I am! *Sniffs his hands.* Sitting in Elmira in the sun with you, and your scent still on my hands! God!— all the different ways there are to try to be real! —I don't know the connection, but when I turned twenty I sold three poems to *The New Yorker* and a story to *Harper's,* and the first thing I bought was a successful blue suit to impress my father how real I was even though a writer. He ran an appetizer store on Fortieth Street and Ninth Avenue. *Grinning, near laughter.* And he sees the suit and says, "How much you pay?" And I said, "Twenty-nine-fifty," thinking I'd got a terrific bargain. And he says, "Pray God keep an eye on you the rest of your life."

LEAH, *laughs:* That's awful!

LYMAN: No!—it spurred me on! *Laughs.* He had two pieces of wisdom—never trust anybody, and never forgive. Funny, it's like magic, I simply can't trace how we got into bed.

LEAH, *a glance at her watch:* I really have to get back to the office.—But is Lyman an Albanian name?

LYMAN: Lyman's the judge's name in Worcester, Massachusetts, who gave my father his citizenship. Felt is short for Feltman, my mother's name, because my father's was unpronounceable and they wanted a successful American for a son.

LEAH: Then your mother was Jewish.

LYMAN: And the source of all my conflicts. In the Jewish heart is a lawyer and a judge, in the Albanian a bandit defying the government with a knife.

LEAH: What a surprise you are! *She stands, and he does.*

LYMAN: Being so silly?

LEAH: Being so interesting, and in the insurance business.

LYMAN, *taking her hand:* When was the moment?—I'm just curious.

LEAH: I don't know . . . I guess at the conference table I suddenly thought, "He's basically talking to me." But then I figured, this is probably why he's such a great salesman, because everybody he talks to feels loved.

LYMAN: You know?—I've never before with a Jewish girl.

LEAH: Well, you're my first Albanian.

LYMAN: There's something venerable in your eyes. Not old—ancient. Like our peoples.

LEAH, *touching his cheek:* Take care, dear.

LYMAN, *as she passes before him to leave, he takes her hand:* Why do I feel I know nothing about you?

LEAH, *shrugs, smiles:* Maybe you weren't listening . . . which I don't mind if it's in a good cause.

LYMAN, *letting go of her hand:* I walk in the valley of your thighs. *She laughs, gives him a quick kiss.* When you move away now, would you turn back to me for a moment?

LEAH, *amused:* Sure, why?

LYMAN, *half-kidding in his romanticism:* I have to take a small commuter plane and if I die I want that vision as I go down—

LEAH, *backing away with a wave:* 'Bye, Lyman . . .

LYMAN: Can I ask who that fellow was banging on your apartment door?

LEAH, *caught off-guard:* Somebody I used to go with . . . he was angry, that's all.

LYMAN: Are you afraid of him?

LEAH, *shrugs in an accepted uncertainty:* See you, dear.

She turns and walks a few yards, then halts and turns her head to look back at him over her shoulder. She exits.

LYMAN: Beautiful. *Alone:* Miraculous. *Thinks for a moment.* Still . . . was it really all *that* great? *Takes out a cell phone, troubled.* Theo?—hi, darling, I'm just about to take off. Oh, definitely, it has the makings of a much bigger operation; had a talk with Aetna's chief rep up here, and she's agreed to take us on, so I'll probably be spending more time here. —Yes, a woman; she's got a great agency, I might try to buy into her. —Listen, dear, how about you flying up here and we rent a car and drive through Cherry Valley—it's bursting into bloom now! —Oh, I forgot; no-no, you'd better go to your meeting then; it's okay; no, it just suddenly hit me how quickly it's all going by and . . . You ever have the feeling that you never *really* got to know anybody?

She never has; he resents it, and a sharpness enters his voice.

Well, yes, I do feel that sometimes, very much; sometimes I feel I'm going to vanish without a trace, Theo! *Unhappily now, with hidden anger, the romance gone.* Theo, dear, it's nothing against you, I only meant that with all the analysis and the novels and the Freuds we're still as opaque and unknowable as some line of statues in a church wall. *He hangs up. Now a light strikes the cast on the bed. He moves to it and looks down at himself. Bessie, Theo, and Leah are standing motionless around the bed and Tom is off to the one side, observing. Lyman slowly lifts his arms and raises his face like a suppliant.* We're all in a cave . . . *The three women now begin to move, ever so slightly at first; their heads are turning as they appear to be searching for the sight of something far away or overhead or on the floor.*

. . . where we entered to make love or money or fame. It's dark in here, as dark as sleep, and each one moves blindly, searching for another, to touch, hoping to touch and afraid; and hoping, and afraid.

As he speaks, the women and Tom move in a crisscrossing path, just missing one another, spreading farther and farther across the stage until one by one they disappear. Lyman has moved above the bed where his cast lies.

So now . . . now that we're here . . . what are we going to say?

BLACKOUT.

ACT TWO

SCENE ONE

The hospital waiting room. Tom is seated with Theo.

TOM: Really, Theo, I wish you'd let Bessie take you back to the city.

THEO: Please stop repeating that! *Slight pause.* I need to talk to him . . . I'll never see him again. I can't simply walk away. Is my head trembling?

TOM: A little, maybe. Should you let one of the doctors look at you?

THEO: I'll be all right, my family has a tendency to tremors, I've had it for years when I'm tense. What time is it?

TOM: Give them a few minutes more. —You seem pale.

THEO, *pressing fingers against her temples to steady herself:* When you spoke with this woman . . . was there any feeling about . . . what she has in mind?

TOM: She's as much in shock as you. The child was her main concern.

THEO: Really? I wouldn't have thought so.

TOM: Oh, I think he means everything to her.

THEO, *begrudgingly:* Well, that's nice. Messes like this are basically comical, aren't they—until you come to the children. I'm very worried about Bessie. She lies there staring at the ceiling. She can hardly talk without starting to weep. He's been her . . . her world. *She begins to fill up.* You're right, I think I'll go. It just seemed unfinished, somehow . . . but maybe it's better to leave it this way . . . *Starts for her bag, stops.* I don't know what to do. One minute I could kill him, the next I wonder if some . . . aberration got into him . . .

Leah enters. They did not expect to see each other. A momentary pause. Leah sits.

LEAH: Good afternoon.

TOM: Good afternoon.

Awkward silence.

LEAH, *asking:* He's not in his room?

THEO, *as it is difficult for her to address Leah, she turns to her slowly:* They're treating his eye.

LEAH: His eye?

TOM: It's nothing serious, he tried to climb out his window. Probably in his sleep. His eyelid was slightly scratched by a rhododendron.

THEO, *making a stab at communication:* He must not have realized he's on the ground floor.

Short pause.

LEAH: Hm! That's interesting, because a friend of ours, Ted Colby, called last night—he's a commander of the state police here. They'd put up a wooden barrier across the Mount Morgan road when it got so icy; and he thinks Lyman moved the barrier aside.

TOM: How could they know it was him?

LEAH: There was only one set of tire tracks.

THEO: Oh my God.

LEAH: He's worried about him. They're good friends, they go hunting together.

THEO: Lyman hunts?

LEAH: Oh sure. *Theo shakes her head incredulously.* But I can't imagine him in that kind of depression, can you?

TOM: Actually . . . yes, I think I can.

LEAH: Really. He's always seemed so . . . up with me, and happy. *Theo glances from her, irked, then away. Leah glances at her watch.* I just have to settle some business with him for a few minutes, I won't be in your way.

THEO: *My* way? You're free to do anything you like, as far as I'm concerned.

LEAH, *slightly taken aback:* Yes . . . the same with me . . . in your case. *Beat.* I mean as far as I'm concerned. *The hostility turns her to look at her watch again.* I want to tell you . . . I almost feel worse for you, somehow, than for myself.

THEO, *gives a hard laugh:* Why! Do I seem *that* old? *The second rebuff stiffens Leah.* I shouldn't have said that. I apologize. I'm exhausted.

LEAH, *letting it pass:* How is your daughter?—she still here?

THEO, *a hostile color despite everything:* In the motel. She's devastated.

TOM: Your boy taking it all right?

LEAH: No, it's wracked him, it's terrible. *To Theo:* I thought Lyman might have some idea how to deal with him, the kid's always idolized him so. I'm really at my wits' end.

THEO, *bitterly angry, but contained:* We are his dust; we billow up behind his steps and settle again when he passes by. Billie Holiday . . . *She touches her forehead.* I can't recall when she died, it's quite a while, isn't it.

TOM: Billie Holiday? Why?

Tom and Leah observe, puzzled, as Theo stares in silence. Then . . .

LEAH: Why don't I come back in a couple of hours—I've got a two o'clock conference call and it's getting a bit late . . . *She stands, goes to Theo, and, extending her hand:* Well, if we don't meet again . . .

THEO, *touching her hand briefly, hostility momentarily overcome:* . . . Do you understand this?

LEAH: It's baffling. He's raced the Mount Morgan road, he knows what it's like, even in summer.

THEO: Raced? You mean cars?

LEAH: Sure. He has a Lotus and a Z. He had a Ferrari, but he totaled it. *Theo turns and stares into space, stunned.* I was thinking before . . .

THEO: He's always been terrified of speed; he never drives over sixty . . .

LEAH: . . . He reminds me of a frog . . .

THEO: A frog?

LEAH: . . . I mean you never know when you look at a frog whether it's the same one you just saw or a different one. *To Tom:* When you talk to him—the television is hounding us; he really has to make a definite statement to stop all this stupid speculation.

THEO: What speculation?

LEAH: You've seen the *Daily News*, haven't you?

THEO: What!

LEAH: We're both on the front page with a headline . . .

TOM, *to Theo, placating:* It's unimportant . . .

THEO, *to Leah:* What's the headline?

LEAH: "Who gets Lyman?"

THEO: How dare they!

TOM: Don't be upset. *To Leah:* I'll get a statement from him this afternoon . . .

LEAH: Goodbye, Mrs. . . . *Stops herself; a short laugh.* I was going to call you Mrs. Felt, but . . . *Correcting again.* . . . Well you are, aren't you—I guess I'm the one who's not! I'll come by about three or so. *Leah exits.*

THEO: She wants him back, doesn't she.

TOM: Why?

THEO, *gives her little laugh:* Didn't you hear it?—she's the one he was happy with!

TOM: Oh, I don't think she meant . . .

THEO, *her fierce competitiveness aroused:* That's *all* she meant.
—I pity her, though, with such a young child. *She fumes in
silence. Can* it have been suicide?

TOM: Frankly, I'd almost hope so, in a way.

THEO: You mean it would indicate a moral conscience?

TOM: Yes. —But I'm wondering . . . maybe he just wanted
to change his life; become a completely different person . . .

THEO, *stares for a moment:* . . . Maybe not so different.

TOM: How do you mean?

THEO, *a long hesitation:* I don't know why I'm still trying to
protect him—he tried to kill me once.

TOM: You're not serious.

*Lyman appears in sunlight in swim trunks, inhaling deeply on a
boat deck. She begins walking toward him.*

THEO: Oh yes! I didn't know this woman existed then, but I
see now it was just about the time they had either married
or were on the verge. *As she moves toward Lyman, her coat
slides off, revealing her in a swimsuit.* ★ He seemed very strange,
unreal. We'd gone for a two-day sail off Montauk . . .

Lyman is doing breathing exercises.

★ This can be played without costume change.

LYMAN: The morning mist rising from the sea is always like the first day of the world . . . the "oysterygods and the visigods . . ."

Theo enters into Lyman's acting area.

THEO: *Finnegans Wake.*

LYMAN: I'll get the weather. *Kneels, tunes a radio; static.* Is that a new suit? It's sexy as hell.

THEO: Two years ago. You bought it for me in San Diego.

LYMAN, *mimes a pistol to his head:* Bang.

ANNOUNCER, *voice-over:* ˙ . . . Due to the unusually warm spring tides there've been several shark sightings off Montauk . . . one is reported to be twelve to fourteen feet long . . . *Heavy static intervenes; Lyman mimes switching the radio off.*

LYMAN: Jesus.

THEO: Oh that's ridiculous, it's only May! I'm going in for a dip . . . *She looks out over the ocean.*

LYMAN: But the radio man said . . .

THEO: Nonsense. I've sailed around here since my childhood, and so did my grandparents—there are never sharks until July if at all, the water's much too cold. Come in with me?

LYMAN: I'm the Mediterranean type—we're unreliable and hate cold water. I know I shouldn't say this, Theo, but how you can hang on to your convictions in the face of a report like that . . . just seems . . . I don't know—fanatical.

THEO, *with a hard, determined laugh:* Now that is really un-called for! You're just as stubborn as I am when you're committed to something.

LYMAN: Goddammit, you're right! And I love your convic-tions!—go ahead, I'll keep an eye out.

THEO, *with loving laughter:* You simply can't stand me con-tradicting you, darling, but it's the best exercise for your character.

LYMAN: Right! And a miserable character it is. Into the ocean! *He leaves her side, scans the ocean.*

THEO, *bends for a dive:* On the mark . . . get set . . .

LYMAN, *pointing left:* What's that out there!

THEO: No, sharks always move, that's a log.

LYMAN: Oh right. Okay, jump in.

THEO: I'll run in! Wait, let me warm up. *Backs up to make a run for it.* Join me! Come on.

LYMAN: I can't, dear, I fear death.

She is behind him, running in place. His back is to her and his eye catches sight of something toward the right front; his mouth opens, eyes staring in horror following the moving shark. She bends to start her run.

THEO: Okay, one . . . and a two . . . and a . . . three! *She runs and as she comes abreast of him he suddenly, at the last moment, reaches out and stops her at the edge.*

LYMAN: Stop!

He points front; she looks, horror rising on her face as their eyes follow the fish.

THEO: My God, the *size* of him! Ahhh . . . ! *She bursts into tears of released terror; he takes her into his arms.*

LYMAN: Honey, when are you going to trust something I say!

THEO: Oh, I'm going to be sick . . . !

About to vomit, she bends and rushes into darkness. Lights go out on Lyman and up on Tom in the waiting room; he is staring straight ahead, listening. The light widens and finds Theo standing in her fur coat.

TOM: That sounds like he saved you.

THEO: Yes, I've always tried to think of it that way, too, but I have to face everything, now—*coming downstage; newly distressed by the memory*—it was not quite at the top of his voice. I mean, it wasn't . . .

Light flares up on Lyman in his trunks. At top voice and in horror he shouts . . .

LYMAN: Stop! *He stands mesmerized looking at the shark below. Blackout on Lyman.*

THEO: It was more like . . .

Lights flare up again on Lyman, and he merely semi-urgently—as he did in the scene—shouts . . .

LYMAN: Stop.

Blackout on Lyman.

THEO: I tell you he was on the verge of letting me go.

TOM: Come on, Theo, you can't really believe that. I mean, how could you have gone on living with him?

THEO: How I've gone on? *A bitter and embarrassed smile.* Well, we did have two serious breakups and . . . months have gone by without . . . relations. *Gradually becomes furious.* No, damnit, I'm not going to evade this anymore. —Maybe I've gone on because I'm corrupt, Tom. I certainly wasn't once, but who knows, now? He's rich, isn't he? And vastly respected, and what would I do with myself alone? Why does anybody stay together, once they realize who they're with? *Suddenly livid.* What the hell am I hanging around here for? This is the stupidest thing I've ever done in my life! *Indignantly grabs her bag.*

TOM: You love him, Theo. *Physically stops her.* Please go home, will you? And give it a few weeks before you decide anything? *She stifles a sob as he embraces her.* I know how crazy this sounds, but part of him worships you. I'm sure of it.

THEO, *suddenly screams in his face:* I hate him! I hate him! *She is rigid, pale, and he grips her shoulders to steady her. A pause.* I must lie down. We'll probably go back to the city tonight. But call me if he wakes up. —It's so hard to just walk away without knowing what happened. —Or maybe I should just leave . . . *She passes her hand across her brow.* Do I look strange?

TOM: Just tired. Come, I'll find you a cab.

THEO: It's only a few blocks, I need the air. *Starting off, turns back.* Amazing how beautiful the country still is up here. Like nothing bad had ever happened in the world. *She exits.*

Alone, Tom stands staring into space, arms folded, trying to figure out an approach.

BLACKOUT.

SCENE TWO

Lyman's room. He is deeply asleep, snoring placidly at first. Now he starts muttering.

NURSE: Why'n't you take some time off? You do more work asleep than most of us awake. You ought to come up ice fishing with us sometime, that'll slow you down.

Nurse goes out. Now there is a tensing up, he is groaning in his sleep. Leah and Theo appear on either side of him, but on elevated platforms, like two stone deities; they are in kitchen aprons, wifely ribbons tying up their hair. But there is something menacing about their deathly stillness as the sepulchral dream-light finds them, motionless in this tableau. After a long moment they reanimate. As in life they are reserved, each measuring herself against the other. Their manner of speaking is godlike, deathly.

THEO: I wouldn't mind it at all if you did some of the cooking, I'm not all that super.

LEAH, *generously:* I hear you make good desserts, though.

THEO: Apple cobbler, yes; gingerbread with whipped cream. *Gaining confidence.* And exceptional waffles for breakfast, with real maple syrup, although he's had to cut out the sausages.

LEAH: I can do potato pancakes and segadina goulash.

THEO, *disapproving:* And all that paprika?

LEAH: It has to be blended in, of course.

THEO, *at a loss, sensing defeat:* Ah, blended in! I'm afraid I couldn't do something like that.

LEAH, *smiling, brutally pressing her advantage:* Oh yes, blended in and really blended *in!* And my gefilte fish is feather-light. *Clapping her cupped palms together.* I wet my hands and keep patting it till it shapes up just perfect!

THEO, *struggling, at a loss:* He does love my glazed ham. Yes!—and my boiled tongue. *A sudden bright idea.* Custard!

LEAH, *generously:* You can do all the custard and glazed ham and I'll do all the gefilte fish and goulash . . . *and* the blending in.

THEO: But may I do *some?* Once or twice a month, perhaps?

LEAH: Let's leave it up to him—some months you can do more . . .

THEO: Yes!—and some months you.

LEAH: 'Kay! Would you wash out my panties?

THEO: Certainly. As long as he tells me my lies.

LEAH: Good! Then you'll have your lies and I'll have mine!

THEO AND LEAH: Hurrah for the menu!

LEAH, *filled with admiration:* You certainly have class!

Lyman chuckles in his sleep as they emerge from their matronly costumes, now dressed in sexy black tight-fitting body stockings and high heels and, slithering toward each other, kiss, turn toward the bed and as he laughs suddenly raise long daggers and chop at him again and again. He is shouting and writhing as Nurse rushes in and the women disappear.

NURSE: All right now, let's come back, dear, come on back . . .

He stops struggling and opens his eyes.

LYMAN: Wah. Oh. What dreams. God, how I'd like to be dead.

NURSE: Don't start feeling sorry for yourself; you know what they say—come down off the cross, they need the wood.

LYMAN: I'm suffocating, can't you open a window?

NURSE: Not anymore, I can't.

LYMAN: Huh? Oh listen, that's ridiculous, I wasn't really trying to climb out . . .

NURSE: Well, you did a pretty good imitation. Your lawyer's asking can he come in . . .

LYMAN: I thought he'd gone back to New York. I look terrible?

NURSE, *swabbing his face and hands:* You takin' it too hard. Be different if you deserted those women, but anybody can see how well taken care of they are. . . .

LYMAN: Go on, you don't kid me, Logan—underneath all this cool you know you're as shocked as hell.

NURSE: Go on, brush your teeth. *As he does:* The last shock I had come off a short in my vacuum cleaner . . . *he laughs, then groans in pain.* One thing I *have* been wondering, though.

LYMAN: What've you been wondering?

NURSE: Whatever got into you to actually marry that woman?—man as smart as you?

LYMAN: Were you talking about ice before?

NURSE: Ice? Oh, you mean . . . ya, we go ice fishing on the lake, me, my husband, and my boy—you're remembering a lot better now.

LYMAN, *staring:* Not being married is going to feel very strange—like suddenly your case has been dismissed and you don't have to be in court anymore.

NURSE: Don't you talk bad about those women; they don't look mean to me.

LYMAN: Why I married her? —I'm very attracted to women who smell like fruit; Leah smelled like a pink, ripe cantaloupe. And when she smiled, her clothes seemed to drop off. I'd never been so jealous. I swear, if a hundred women walked past me on a sidewalk I could pick out the clack of Leah's heels. I even loved lying in bed listening to the quiet splash of her bathwater. And of course slipping into her pink cathedral . . .

NURSE: You have the dirtiest mind I ever seen on an educated man.

LYMAN: I couldn't lose her, Logan, and that's the best reason to marry anybody, unless you're married already.

NURSE: I'll get your lawyer, okay? *He seems suddenly overcome; weeps.* Now don't you start that cryin' again . . .

LYMAN: It's just my children . . . you can't imagine how they respected me . . . *Bracing himself.* But nobody's any better, goddammit!

Tom enters.

TOM: May I come in?

LYMAN, *uncertainly, trying to read Tom:* Hi! I thought you'd gone back—something happen?

TOM: Can we talk?

Nurse exits.

LYMAN: If you can bear it. *Grins.* You despise me, Tom?

TOM: I'm still staggering. I don't know what to think.

LYMAN: Sure you do, but that's okay. *His charming grin.* So, what's up?

TOM: I've been discussing things with the women . . .

LYMAN: I thought I told you—or did I?—just give them what they want. Within reason, I mean.

TOM: I really believe Theo'd like to find a way to forgive you.

LYMAN: Impossible!

TOM: She's a great spirit, Lyman.

LYMAN: . . . Not that great; I'd have to live on my knees for the rest of my life.

TOM: Maybe not—if you were clear about yourselves . . .

LYMAN: I'm pretty clear now—I'm a selfish son of a bitch. But I have loved the truth.

TOM: And what's the truth?

LYMAN: A man can be faithful to himself or to other people—but not to both. At least not happily. We all know this, but it's immoral to admit that the first law of life is betrayal; why else did those rabbis pick Cain and Abel to open the Bible? Cain felt betrayed by God, so he betrayed Him and killed his brother.

TOM: But the Bible doesn't end there, does it.

LYMAN: Jesus Christ? I can't worship self-denial; it's just not true for me. We're all ego, kid, ego plus an occasional heartfelt prayer.

TOM: Then why'd you bother building one of the most socially responsible companies in America?

LYMAN: The truth? I did that twenty-five years ago, when I was a righteous young man; but I am an unrighteous middle-aged man now, so all I have left is to try not to live with too many lies. *Suddenly collapsing within.* —Why must I see them? . . . What can I say to them? Christ, if I could only lose consciousness! *Rocking side to side in anguish.* . . . Advise me, Tom, tell me something.

TOM: Maybe you ought to give up trying to seem so strong.

Slight pause.

LYMAN: What do you want me to say, I'm a loser?

TOM: Well, right now, aren't you?

LYMAN: No, goddammit! A loser has lived somebody else's life, I've lived my own; crappy as it may seem, it's mine. —And I'm no worse than anybody else! —Now answer that, and don't kid me.

TOM: All right, I won't kid you; I think you've done these women terrible harm.

LYMAN: You do.

TOM: If you want to get off this dime you're on I'd begin by confronting the damage I'd done——I think you've raked Theo's soul.

LYMAN: I've also given her an interesting life, a terrific daughter, and made her very rich. I mean, exactly what harm are you talking about?

TOM: Lyman, you deceived her . . .

LYMAN, *fury overtaking him:* But she couldn't have had all that if I hadn't deceived her!——you know as well as I that nobody could live with Theo for more than a month without some relief! I've suffered at least as much as she has in this marriage!

TOM, *demurring:* Well . . .

LYMAN: . . . Now listen, you want the rock-bottom truth?—— I curse the day I ever laid eyes on her and I don't *want* her forgiveness!

TOM: For Pete's sake, don't get angry . . .

LYMAN: I ever tell you how we met?——let's stop pretending this marriage was made in heaven, for Christ's sake!——I was hitchhiking back from Cornell; nineteen innocent years of age; I'm standing beside the road with my suitcase and I go behind a bush. This minister sees the suitcase and stops, gives me a ride, and I end up at an Audubon Society picnic, where lo and behold, I meet his daughter, Theodora.——Had I taken that suitcase with me behind the bush I'd never have met her!——And serious people are still talking about the moral purpose of the universe!

TOM: Give or take a bad patch or two, you've had the best marriage of anyone I've ever met.

LYMAN, *with a sigh:* I know. —Look, we're all the same; a man is a fourteen-room house—in the bedroom he's asleep with his intelligent wife, in his living room he's rolling around with some bare-assed girl, in the library he's paying his taxes, in the yard he's raising tomatoes, and in the cellar he's making a bomb to blow it all up. And nobody's different . . . Except you, maybe. Are you?

TOM: I don't raise tomatoes . . . Listen, the TV is flogging the story and it's humiliating for the women; let's settle on a statement and be done with it. What do you want?

LYMAN: What I always wanted; both of them.

TOM: Be serious . . .

LYMAN: I know these women and they still love me! It's only what they think they're *supposed* to feel that's confusing them. —Do I sound crazy?

TOM: Listen, I forgot to tell you—Jeff Huddleston called me this morning; heard it on the radio; he insists you resign from the board.

LYMAN: Not on your life! That fat fraud—Jeff Huddleston's got a woman stashed in Trump Tower and two in L.A.

TOM: *Huddleston!*

LYMAN: He offered to loan me one once! Huddleston has more outside ass than a Nevada whorehouse!

TOM: But he doesn't marry them.

LYMAN: Right!—in other words, what I really violated was the law of hypocrisy.

TOM: Unfortunately that's the one that operates.

LYMAN: Not with me, baby! I may be a bastard but I am not a hypocrite! I am not quitting my company! What's Leah saying . . . anything?

TOM: She's stunned. But frankly, I'm not sure she's out of the question either . . . if that's the move you wanted to make.

LYMAN, *deeply touched:* What size these women have! *Weeping threatens again.* Oh Tom, I'm lost!

Bessie and Theo enter. Theo stands beside his bed staring at him without expression. Bessie doesn't so much as look at him. After a long moment . . .

Downing fear: My God, Theo—thank you . . . I mean for coming. I didn't expect you . . .

She sits down in a potent silence. Bessie stands, fiercely aloof. He is openly and awkwardly ashamed.

Hi, Bessie.

BESSIE: I'm here for her sake, she wanted to say something to you. *Hurrying her along.* Mother?

But Theo takes no notice, staring at Lyman with a fixed, unreadable smile. After a long, awkward moment . . .

LYMAN, *to fill the void:* How are you feeling today? I hear you were . . .

THEO, *dead flat, cutting him off:* I won't be seeing you again, Lyman.

LYMAN, *despite everything, a bit of a blow—slight pause:* Yes. Well . . . I guess there's no use in apologizing. . . . But I am sorry, Theo.

THEO: I can't leave my life lying all over the floor like this.

LYMAN: I'll talk about anything you like.

THEO: I seem confused but I'm not; there's just so much that I . . . that I don't want bottled up in me anymore.

LYMAN: Sure, I understand.

THEO: —Do you remember that young English instructor whose wife walked out on him—his advice to you about sex?

LYMAN: An English instructor? At Cornell, you mean?

THEO: "Bend it in half," he said, "and tie a rubber band around it."

LYMAN, *laughing, a little alarmed:* Oh sure, Jim Donaldson!

THEO: Everyone used to laugh at that.

LYMAN: *Her smile is empty, his charm desperate.* Right! "Bend it in half and . . ." *Continues a strained chuckling.*

THEO, *cutting him off:* I *hated* you laughing at that; it showed a vulgar and disgusting side of you. I was ashamed . . . for you and for myself.

LYMAN, *brought up short:* I see. But that's so long ago, Theo . . .

THEO: I want to tell you that I nearly ended it right then and there, but I thought I was too inexperienced to make a judgment. But I was right—you *were* a vulgar, unfeeling man, and you are still.

Anxiously, Lyman glances over to Bessie for help or explanation of this weirdness.

LYMAN: I see. Well, I guess our whole life was a mistake then. *Angered but attempting charm.* But I made a good living.

BESSIE: Please, Mother, let's go, he's mocking you, can't you hear it?

LYMAN, *flaring up:* Must I not defend myself? Please go ahead, Theo, I understand what you're saying, and it's okay, it's what you feel.

THEO, *seemingly relaxed:* —What was the name of the river, about half an hour's walk past the Chemistry building?

LYMAN, *puzzled—is she mad?:* What river?

THEO: Where we went skinny-dipping with those geologists and their girls?

LYMAN, *at a loss for a moment:* Oh, you mean graduation night!

THEO: ... The whole crowd swimming naked at the falls ... and the girls all laughing in the darkness ... ?

LYMAN, *starting to smile but still uncomprehending:* Oh sure ... that was a great night!

THEO: I straddled you, and over your shoulder ... did I dream this? I recall a white wall of limestone, rising straight out of the river ... ?

LYMAN: That's right, Devonian. It was full of fossils.

THEO: Yes! Beetle imprints, worm tracks, crustacea fifty million years old going straight up like a white temple wall ... and we floated around below, like two frogs attached in the darkness ... our wet eyelashes touching.

LYMAN: Yes. It was beautiful. I'm glad you remember it that way.

THEO: Of course I do; I was never a Puritan, Lyman, it is simply a question of taste—that night was inspiring.

LYMAN: Well, I never had taste, we both know that. But I won't lie to you, Theo—taste to me is what's left of life after people can't screw anymore.

THEO: You should have told me that thirty years ago.

LYMAN: I didn't know it thirty years ago.

THEO: And do you remember what you said as we floated there?

LYMAN, *hesitates:* Yes.

THEO: You couldn't.

LYMAN: I said, "What could ever come between us?" Correct?

THEO, *surprised, derailed:* . . . But did you mean that then? Please tell me the truth, it's important to me.

LYMAN, *affected:* Yes, I meant it.

THEO: Then . . . when did you begin to fool me?

LYMAN: Please don't go on anymore . . .

THEO: I am trying to pinpoint when my life died. That's not unreasonable, is it?

LYMAN: From my heart, Theo, I ask your pardon.

THEO: —When did Billie Holiday die?

LYMAN, *perplexed:* Billie Holiday?—oh I don't know, ten, twelve years ago? Why?

Theo goes silent, staring into space. He is suddenly weeping at the sight of her suffering.

Why do you want to know about Billie?

BESSIE: All right, Mother, let's go, huh?

LYMAN: I think it might be better if she talked it out . . .

BESSIE: No one is interested in what you think. *To Theo:* I want you to come now!

LYMAN: Have mercy!

BESSIE: You talking mercy?!

LYMAN: For her, not me! Don't you hear what she's trying to say?—she loved me!

BESSIE: How can you listen to this shit!

LYMAN: How dare you! I gave you a damned fine life, Bessie!

BESSIE: You have nothing to say anymore, you are nonsense!

THEO: Please, dear!—wait outside for a few minutes. *Bessie, seeing her adamance, strides out.* You've torn out her heart. *Ly-*

man turns away trying not to weep. Was there some pleasure in making a fool of me? Why couldn't you have told me about this woman?

LYMAN: I did try, many times, but . . . I guess it sounds crazy, but . . . I just couldn't bear to lose you.

THEO: But—*with sudden, near-hysterical intensity*—you were lying to me every day all these nine or ten years—what could you possibly lose?

LYMAN, *determined not to flinch:* . . . Your happiness.

THEO: *My* happiness! In God's name what are you talking about!

LYMAN: Only the truth can help us, Theo—I think you were happier in those last years than ever in our marriage— you feel that, don't you?

She doesn't contradict.

May I tell you why? Because I was never bored being with you.

THEO: You'd been bored with me?

LYMAN: Same as you'd been bored with me, dear . . . I'm talking about—you know—just normal marital boredom.

She seems obtuse to this, so he tries to explain.

You know, like at dinner—when I'd repeat some inane story you'd heard a thousand times . . . ? Like my grandfather losing three fingers under the Ninth Avenue trolley . . . ?

THEO: But I loved that story! I was *never* bored with you . . . stupid as that was.

LYMAN, *now she just seems perverse:* Theo, you were bored—it's no sin! Same as I was when, for instance, you'd start telling people for the ten thousandth time that . . . *his charming laugh* . . . as a minister's daughter you were not permitted to climb a tree and show off your panties?

THEO, *sternly resisting his charm:* But I think that story describes a kind of society that has completely disappeared! That story has historical importance!

LYMAN, *the full agony:* That story is engraved in my flesh! . . . And I beg you, don't make this a moral dilemma. It is just common domestic tedium, dear, it is life, and there's no other woman I know who has the honesty and strength to accept it as life—if you wanted to!

THEO, *a pause; above her confusion, she is striving desperately to understand:* And why do you say I was happier in these last years?

LYMAN: Because you could see my contentment, and I was content . . .

THEO: Because she . . . ?

LYMAN: Because whenever you started with your panties again I could still find you lovable, knowing that story was not going to be my entire and total fate till the day I died.

THEO: . . . Because she was waiting for you.

LYMAN: Right.

THEO: You were never bored with *her?*

LYMAN: Oh God yes! Sometimes even more than with you.

THEO, *with quick, intense, hopeful curiosity:* Really! And what then?

LYMAN: Then I would thank my luck that I had you to come back to. —I know how hard this is to understand, Theo.

THEO: No-no . . . I guess I've always known it.

LYMAN: What.

THEO: You are some kind of . . . of giant clam.

LYMAN: Clam?

THEO: Waiting on the bottom for whatever happens to fall from the ocean into your mouth; you are simply a craving, and that craving you call love. You are a kind of monster, and I think you even know it, don't you. I can almost pity you, Lyman. *She turns to leave.* I hope you make a good recovery. It's all very clear now, I'm glad I stayed.

LYMAN: It's amazing—the minute the mystery of life appears, you think everything's cleared up.

THEO: There's no mystery to me, you have never loved anyone!

LYMAN: Then explain to yourself how this worthless, loveless, treacherous clam could have single-handedly made two such different women happier than they'd ever been in their lives!

THEO: Really! *Laughs, ending in a near-scream.* Really and truly *happy?!*

LYMAN: . . . In fact, if I dared admit the whole idiotic truth, the only one who suffered these past nine years— was *me!*

An enormous echoing roar fills the theater—the roar of a lion. Light rises on Bessie looking front through field glasses; she is wearing shorts and a pith helmet and khaki safari jacket.

THEO: *You suffering?*—oh dear God save us!

She is trying to sustain her bitter laughter and moves toward Bessie, and as she enters Bessie's area Theo's laughter dies off and she takes a pith helmet out of a picnic basket and puts it on. Lyman, slipping out of bed at the same time, follows Theo. There is no dialogue break.

LYMAN: . . . What would you call it, then—having to look into your innocent, loving faces, when I knew the hollowness your happiness was based on? That isn't suffering?

He takes his place beside the two women, looking in the same direction out front, shading his eyes. With no break in dialogue . . .

BESSIE, *looking through field glasses:* Good heavens, is he going to mount her *again?*

LYMAN: They don't call him the king of the beasts for nothing, honey.

BESSIE: Poor thing, how patient she is.

THEO, *taking the glasses from her:* Oh come, dear, she's not *only* patient.

BESSIE, *spreading a tablecloth and picnic things on the ground:* But it's only once every half a year, isn't it?

LYMAN: Once that we *know* about.

THEO, *helping to spread the picnic:* Oh no, they're marvelously loyal couples.

LYMAN: No, dear, lions have harems—you're thinking of storks.

BESSIE, *offering an egg:* Daddy?

LYMAN, *sitting—happily eating:* I love you in those helmets, you look like two noble ladies on safari.

THEO, *stretching out on the ground:* The air here! The silence. These hills.

BESSIE: Thanks for bringing me, Daddy. I wish Harold could have been here. —Why do you look sad?

LYMAN: Just thinking. *To Theo:* About monogamy—why you suppose we think of it as a higher form of life? *She turns up to him . . . defensively . . .* I mean I was just wondering.

THEO: Well, it implies an intensification of love.

LYMAN: How about that, Bess? You had a lot of boyfriends before Harold, didn't you?

BESSIE: Well . . . yes, I guess it is more intense with one.

LYMAN: But how does that make it a higher form?

THEO: Monogamy strengthens the family; random screwing undermines it.

LYMAN: But as one neurotic to another, what's so good about strengthening the family?

THEO: Well, for one thing it enhances liberty.

BESSIE: Liberty? Really?

THEO: The family disciplines its members; when the family is weak the state has to move in; so the stronger the family the fewer the police. And that is why monogamy is a higher form.

LYMAN: Jesus, did you just make that up? *To Bessie:* Isn't she marvelous? I'm giving her an A-plus!

THEO, *happily hurt:* Oh shut up.

LYMAN: But what about those Muslims? They're very big on stable families but a lot of them have two or three wives.

THEO: But only one is really the *wife.*

LYMAN: Not according to my father—they often had two main women in Albania, one to run the house and the other for the bed. But they were both serious wives.

THEO: Your father's sociology was on a par with his morals. A wife to your father was a walking dish towel.

LYMAN, *laughs, to Bessie:* Your mother is a classical woman, you know why?

BESSIE, *laughing delightedly:* Why?

LYMAN: Because she is always clear and consistent and . . .

THEO: . . . Rather boring.

He guffaws warmly, clapping his hands over his head in appreciation.

BESSIE: You are not boring! *Rushing to embrace Theo.* Tell her she is not boring!

LYMAN, *embracing Theo with Bessie:* Theo, please . . . I swear I didn't mean boring!

THEO, *tearfully hurt:* Well I'd rather be boring and clear than cute and stupid!

LYMAN: Who asked you to be cute!—now please don't go on about it.

THEO: I wish I knew how to amuse you! Your eyes have been glazed over since we stepped onto this wretched continent!

LYMAN, *guiltily stretching an awkward embrace toward her:* I *love* this trip, and being with both of you . . . ! Theo, please!—now you are making me guilty!

The lion's roar interrupts and they all look front in shock.

BESSIE: Is he heading here . . . ? Daddy!—he's trotting!

GUIDE'S VOICE, *off, on bullhorn:* You will have to come back to the car, everyone! At once!

LYMAN: Quick! *He pushes both women off.*

BESSIE, *on exiting:* Daddy, come . . . !

THEO, *sensing he is remaining behind:* Lyman . . . ?

LYMAN: Go! *He pushes Theo off, but turns back himself.*

GUIDE'S VOICE: Come back to the car at once, Mr. Felt!

Lion's roar—but closer now. Lyman facing front and the lion, pre-pared to run for it but holding his ground.

Mr. Felt, get back to the car!

Another roar.

LYMAN, *eyes on the lion, shouting toward it with fear's exhilaration:* I *am* happy, yes! That I'm married to Theodora and have Bessie . . . yes, *and Leah, too!*

Another roar!

BESSIE, *from a distance:* Daddy, please come here!

LYMAN: And that I've made a mountain of money . . . yes, and have no impending lawsuits!

BESSIE, *from a distance:* Daddy . . . !

LYMAN, *flinging his words toward the approaching beast, but crouched and ready to flee:* . . . And that I don't sacrifice one day to things I don't believe in—including monogamy, yes!—*arms thrown out, terror-inspired*—I love my life, I am not guilty! I dare you to eat me, son of a bitch!

Immense roar! Wide-eyed, crouched now, and on the very verge of fleeing, he is watching the approaching lion—whose roar, as we now hear, has changed to a rather more relaxed guttural growling, much diminished; and Lyman cautiously straightens up, and now turns triumphantly toward the women offstage. And Bessie flies out and throws her arms around him in ecstatic relief, kissing him.

BESSIE, *looking front:* Daddy, he turned back! What did you do that for!

Theo enters.

THEO: He turned back! *To Lyman:* How did you do that! *To Bessie:* Did you see how he stopped and turned around? *To Lyman:* What happened?

LYMAN: I think I've lost my guilt! I think he sensed it! *Half-laughing.* Maybe lions don't eat happy people!

THEO: What are you talking about?

LYMAN, *staring in wonder:* I tell you his roar hit my teeth like voltage and suddenly it was so clear that . . . *Turns to her.* I've always been happy with you, Theo!—I just somehow couldn't accept it! But I am never going to apologize for my happiness again!—it's a miracle!

THEO, *with tears of gratitude, clasping her hands together prayerfully:* Oh, Lyman! *Rushing to kiss him.* Oh, darling!

LYMAN, *still riding his wave, holding out his hand to her:* What old good friends we are, Theo! Put her there! *She laughs and manfully shakes hands.* What a *person* you are, what a grave and beautiful face you have!

BESSIE: Oh, Daddy, that's so lovely!—you're just marvelous! *She weeps.*

LYMAN: I worship this woman, Bessie! *To Theo:* How the hell are we still together? *To Bessie:* —Do you realize how she must love me to stand for my character?

THEO: Oh, this is what I always saw happening someday!—*a sophisticated laugh*—not with a lion, of course, but exactly this sudden flash of light . . . !

LYMAN: The whole future is clear to me now! We are going to march happily into our late middle age, proudly, heads up! I'm going to build a totally selfish little cottage in the Caribbean and we'll fill it up with all the thick English novels we never got to finish . . . plus Proust!—and I'll buy two mopeds with little baskets on the handlebars for the shopping trips . . .

THEO: I knew it, I knew it!

LYMAN: . . . And I'll spend every day with you—except maybe a week or so a month in the Elmira office!

BESSIE: How fantastic, Mother!

THEO: Thank you, lion! Thank you, Africa! *Turning to him.* Lyman?

LYMAN, *already mentally departing the scene:* . . . Huh? Yes!

THEO: I am all new!

She throws her arms around him, burying her face in his neck. He looks front with an expression of deepening agony.

BESSIE: This has been the most fantastic two weeks of my life! I love you, Daddy!

She rushes to him and with one arm he embraces her, the other around Theo. Tears are starting in his eyes.

Are you weeping?

LYMAN: Just amazement, honey . . . at my luck, I guess. Come, we'd better go back.

Somberly he turns them upstage; lights are changing, growing dimmer, and they walk into the darkness while he remains behind. Dim light reveals the Nurse sitting near the bed.

NURSE: The only thing I don't understand is why you married that woman, a smart man like you.

Lyman stares ahead as Leah appears, isolated in light; she is in her fur coat, exactly as in Act One when she was about to go for an abortion. The Nurse remains in periphery, immobile.

LEAH: Yes, I suppose it could wait a week or so, but . . . really, Lyman, you know you're never going to leave her.

LYMAN: You cancel the operation, okay? And I'm telling her tomorrow.

LEAH: You're telling her what?

LYMAN, *almost holding his breath:* I will not rationalize you away. I have one life! I'm going to ask her for a divorce.

LEAH: My God, Lyman! —But listen, I know your attach-
ment to her . . .

LYMAN, *kisses her hand:* Please keep this baby. Will you? And
stay home and cross your legs, you hear?

LEAH: This is serious?

LYMAN: This is serious. I'm asking her for a divorce.

LEAH: Suddenly . . . why am I not sure I want to be a
mother!—Do I, do you think?

LYMAN: Yes you do, we think!

*Kisses her. They laugh together. He turns to leave; she grasps his
hands and presses them together between hers in a prayerful gesture;
and facing heaven . . .*

LEAH: Please! Some good luck! *To Lyman directly:* Why is
everything so dangerous! *She gives him a violent kiss. She exits
as Theo appears walking toward him; she is hiding something behind her back and smiling lovingly. Lyman looks solemn, prepared
for the showdown.*

LYMAN: Theo, dear . . . There's something I have to tell
you . . .

THEO, *holding out a cashmere sweater:* Happy birthday!

LYMAN, *startled:* Hah? But it's not July, is it!

THEO: But it was so sinfully expensive I needed an excuse. *Putting him into the sweater.* Here . . . straighten it. It's not too big, is it? *Stepping back to admire.* It's georgeous, look in the mirror!

LYMAN: It's beautiful, thank you, dear. But listen, I really have something to . . .

THEO: My God, Lyman, you are simply magnificent! *Linking arms with him and walking in her cumbersome way.* I have another surprise—I got tickets for the Balanchine! And a table at Luigi's afterwards!

LYMAN, *grimly screwing up his courage—and beginning to resent her domination:* I have something to tell you, Theo, why do you make it so hard for me!

THEO: What. *He is paralyzed.* What is it? Has something happened? *Alarmed now.* Lyman!—*asking*—you went for your checkup!

LYMAN, *about to explode:* God's sake, no, it's not that!

THEO: Why is your face so gray? Please, what is it, you look terrified!

He moves away from her and her awful caring, and halts facing front. She remains behind and calls to him from the distance.

—My cousin Wilbur's still at Mass. General, we can go up there together . . . ! Please, darling, don't worry about anything . . . ! What is it, can't you tell me?

In total blockage—both in the past and in the present—he inhales deeply and lets out a gigantic long howl, arms raised, imploring heaven for relief. In effect, it blasts her out of his mind—she goes dark, and he is alone again.

LYMAN, *to himself, facing front:* No guts. That's the whole story. Courage! If I'd been honest for three consecutive minutes . . . No! I know what's wrong with me—I could never stand still for death! Which you've got to do by a certain age, or be ridiculous—you've got to stand there nobly and serene and let death run his tape out your arms and around your belly and up your crotch until he's got you fitted for that last black suit. And I can't, I won't! . . . So I'm left wrestling with this anachronistic energy which . . . *as he leaps onto the bed, covering his left arm, crying out to the world* . . . God has charged me with and I will use it till the dirt is shoveled into my mouth! Life! Life! Fuck death and dying!

Light widens, finding Leah in the present, dressed differently than previously—in her fur coat—standing near the bed with the Nurse, listening to his shouts.

NURSE: Don't be afraid, just wait a minute, he comes out of it. I'm sure he wants to see you.

LEAH, *moving tentatively to the cast:* Lyman? *He looks at her with cloudy recognition.* It's me, Leah.

Nurse exits. Lyman now fully aware of Leah.

LYMAN: Leah! *Turning away from her.* Jesus, what have I done to you!—wait . . . *A moment. He looks around.* Was Theo here?

LEAH: I think she's gone, I just got here.

LYMAN: Oh, Leah, it's sitting on my chest like a bag of cement.

LEAH: What is?

LYMAN: My character.

LEAH: Yes, well . . . it's pretty bad. Listen . . .

LYMAN, *moved:* Thanks for coming. You're a friend.

LEAH: I only came about Benny. *Frustrated, turns away.* He's excited that he has a sister.

LYMAN, *painful admiration:* Oh that dear boy!

LEAH: He's very badly mixed up, Lyman; he's seen us all on TV and the other kids tell him he has two mothers. He sits there and weeps. He keeps asking me are you coming home again. It's twisting my heart. I'm terrified if this isn't settled right it could screw up the rest of his life. *Tears start.* You're his idol, his god, Lyman!

LYMAN: Oh, the wreckage, the wreckage . . .

LEAH: Tell me the truth; whichever it is is okay but I just want to know—do you feel a responsibility or not?

LYMAN, *flaring up, scared as much as indignant:* How can you ask such a thing?

LEAH: Why! That's a reasonable question!

LYMAN: Now listen to me—I know I'm wrong and I'm wrong and I'm wrong but I did not throw you both across my saddle to rape you in my tent! You knew I was married, and you tried to make me love you, so I'm not entirely . . .

LEAH: Lyman, if you're blaming me I'm going to sink through this floor!

LYMAN: I'm talking about truth, not blame—this is not entirely a one-man disaster!

LEAH: It's amazing, the minute you talk about truth you always come out looking better than anyone else!

LYMAN: Now that's unfair!

LEAH, *slight pause:* I want to talk about Benny.

LYMAN: You could bring him tomorrow if you like. But go ahead, we can talk now.

LEAH, *a pause as she settles down:* I'm thinking.

LYMAN: Well stop thinking and bring him!

LEAH, *with a flushed grin:* Incidentally . . . they tell me you spent over an hour with your wife. Are you settling in there again?

LYMAN: All she did was sit there telling me I'm a monster who never loved anybody.

LEAH, *with a hard grin:* And you reassured her otherwise, of course.

LYMAN: Well, I did love her. And you know that better than anybody.

LEAH: What a piece of work you are, Lyman, really—you go falling off a mountain and you still don't understand your hatred for that woman. It's monumental. It's . . . it's *oceanic.*

LYMAN: What the hell is this now!

LEAH: My dear man, in case it slipped your mind, when I was two months pregnant we went to New York and you picked the Carlyle Hotel to stay at—four blocks from your house! "Loved her" . . . good G—!

A window begins to appear upstage with Theo seated in profile, reading a book. He is staring as he emerges from the bed, turning to look up at the window . . . Leah goes on with no pause.

What was all that about if it wasn't hatred!—And walking me past your front window with her sitting there . . . ? You had murder in you and you still do!—probably for me too!

LYMAN, *glancing up at Theo in the window:* But it didn't feel like murder at all. I was dancing the high wire on the edge of the world . . . finally risking everything to find myself! Strolling with you past my house, the autumn breeze, the lingerie in the Madison Avenue shop windows, the swish of . . . wasn't it a taffeta skirt you wore? . . . and my new baby coiled in your belly? —I'd beaten guilt forever! *She is moving toward him, part of his recall. . . . And how languorous* you were, your pregnant glory under the streetlamp!

She takes on the ease of that long-ago stroll, and . . .

LEAH: Is that her?

Lyman looks up at Theo, then at Leah, inspired, alive.

LYMAN: Oh Leah darling, how sexy you look against tall buildings.

LEAH, *with a warm smile, taking his arm:* You're tense, aren't you.

LYMAN: Well, I lived here with her for so many years . . . You know?—I'd love to go in and say hello . . . But I don't have the guts . . .

LEAH: Was she very upset when you told her?

LYMAN, *tragically, but hesitates:* Very, yes.

LEAH: Well, maybe she'll think of marrying again.

LYMAN: Marrying again? *With a glance to the window; loosening her grip on his arm.* I doubt it, somehow.

LEAH, *with an intrigued smile:* Mustn't we touch?

LYMAN, *quickly regaining her arm:* Of course! *They start walking away.*

LEAH: I'd love to meet her sometime . . . just as friends.

LYMAN: You might. *Halts. A strange determination suddenly:* Listen, I'd like to see if I can go in and say hello.

LEAH: Why not! You don't want me to come, do you?

LYMAN: Not just yet. Would you mind a lot?

LEAH: Why! I'm glad that you still have feeling for her.

LYMAN: God, you have balls! I'll see you back at the hotel in twenty minutes, okay?

LEAH: Take your time! I'll play with all that gorgeous underwear you bought. *Touching her belly.* I'm so contented, Lyman!

She turns and walks toward the cast, which lights up. He remains below the window, staring at her departing figure.

LYMAN, *alone:* Why is it, the happier she is the sadder I get? It's this damned *objectivity!*—Why can't I just dive in and swim in my happiness! *Now he looks up at Theo, and his heart sinks. Leaps up with violent determination.* Idiot!—love her! Now that she can't deprive you anymore let love flow to your wise and wonderful wife! *He rushes toward Theo, but then turns away in terror, walking around in a circle and blowing out air and covering his face.* Guilt, burn in hell! *Now he again hurries toward the window . . . which disappears, as she rises, setting her book down, startled.*

THEO: Lyman! —You said Tuesday, didn't you?

He takes her in his arms, kisses her frantically. She is surprised and happy.

LYMAN: What a handsome lady! Theo, you are God's hand-writing.

THEO: Ralph Waldo Emerson.

LYMAN: Someday I'm going to swipe an image you never heard of! *Laughing, in a comradely style, embraces her closely as he takes her to a seat—stoking up a certain excited intimacy here.* Listen, I just hitched a ride down with this pilot in his new Cessna—I have meetings up there starting seven-thirty tomorrow but I just had to astonish you.

THEO: You flew in a small plane *at night?*

LYMAN: That whole fear was guilt, Theo—I thought I *deserved* to crash. But I deserve to live because I am not a bad guy and I love you.

THEO: Well, I'm floating away! When must you go back?

LYMAN: Now.

THEO, *near laughter at the absurdity:* Can't we even chat?

LYMAN: Let me call that I'm on my way. *Dials a phone.*

THEO: I'll drive you to the airport.

LYMAN: No, he's picking me up at the Carlyle . . . Hello?

Lights up on Leah, holding a phone.

LEAH: Darling!

LYMAN: Be there in ten minutes.

LEAH, *puzzled:* Oh? Okay. Why are you calling?

LYMAN: Just to make sure you didn't forget me and took off.

LEAH: Your jealousy is so comforting!—You know, she made a very dignified picture, reading in the window—it was like an Edward Hopper, kind of haunted.

LYMAN: Yes. Well, I'm leaving right now. *Hangs up.*

THEO: You won't forget about dinner Thursday with Leona and Gilbert . . . he's gotten his hearing aid so it won't be so bad.

LYMAN, *with a certain solemnity, taking her hands:* I just had to steal this extra look at you . . . life's so stupidly short, Theo.

THEO, *happily:* Why must death always sit on your shoulder when you've got more life in you than anybody! *Ruffling his hair.* In fact, you're kind of sparkly tonight.

LYMAN, *responding to her acceptance:* Listen, we have time to make love.

THEO, *with a surprised, delighted laugh:* I wish I knew what's come over you!

LYMAN: The realization of what a sweet piece of ass my wife is. *He starts to lead her.*

THEO: I bet it's the new office in Elmira—new beginnings are always so exciting! There's such power in you, Lyman.

LYMAN, *turning her to him, he kisses her mouth:* Yes, we're going to do great business up there! Tell me something—has there ever been a god who was guilty?

THEO: Gods are never guilty, that's why they're gods.

LYMAN: It feels like the moon's in my belly and the sun's in my mouth and I'm shining down on the world. *Laughs with a self-mocking charm.* . . . A regular planetary flashlight! Come! *And laughing in high tension takes her hand and moves her into darkness* . . .

THEO: Oh, Lyman—how wonderfully, endlessly changing you are!

BLACKOUT.

SCENE THREE

Lights up on Leah in hospital room; Lyman is returning to the bed.

LEAH: So you bopped her that night.

LYMAN: What can I say?

LEAH: And when you came back to the hotel, didn't we . . . ?

LYMAN: I couldn't help myself, you both looked absolutely gorgeous! How can that be evil?

LEAH, *with a sigh:* There's just no end to you, is there. —Listen, I came to talk business; I want the house transferred to my name . . .

LYMAN: *What?*

LEAH: . . . Immediately. I know how much feeling you put into it but I want the security for Benny's sake.

LYMAN: Leah, I beg you to wait with that . . .

LEAH: I will not wait with that! And I want my business returned to me.

LYMAN: That'll be complicated—it's many times bigger than when I took it over . . .

LEAH: I want it back! I would have expanded without you! I'm not going to be a *total* fool! I will sue you!

LYMAN, *with a very uncertain grin:* You'd really sue me?

LEAH, *searching in her pocketbook:* I'm not fooling around, Lyman. You've hurt me very deeply . . . *She breaks off, holding back tears. She takes out a sheet of paper.*

LYMAN, *forced to turn from her:* Jesus, how I hate to see you cry.

LEAH: I have something I want you to sign.

LYMAN: To *sign?*

LEAH: It's a quit-claim on the house and my business. Will you read it?

LYMAN: You're not serious.

LEAH: I had Ted Lester draw it up. Here, read it.

LYMAN: I know what a quit-claim is, don't tell me to read a quit-claim. How can you do this?

LEAH: We aren't married and I don't want you making claims on me.

LYMAN: And . . . and what about Benny. You don't mean you're taking Benny from me . . .

LEAH: I . . .

LYMAN: I want you to bring him here tomorrow morning so I can talk to him.

LEAH: Just a minute . . .

LYMAN: No! You're going to bring him, Leah . . .

LEAH: Now you listen to me! I will not allow you to see him until I know what you intend to say to him about all this. I've also been through it with my father's old lawyer and you haven't a legal leg to stand on.

LYMAN: I'll tell him the truth——I love him.

LEAH: You mean it's all right to lie and deceive people you love? He's all I have now, Lyman, I am not going to see him go crazy!

LYMAN: Now you stop that! I did a helluva lot more than lie to him . . .

LEAH, *outpouring:* You lied to him!——why don't you seem to register this? . . . To buy him the pony, and teach him to ski, and take him up in the glider . . . you made him worship you——when you knew what you knew! That was cruelty!

LYMAN: All right, what do you think I should tell him?

LEAH: That you beg his pardon and say he mustn't follow your example because lying to people injures them.

LYMAN: I am not turning myself into a pile of shit in front of my son's face! If I can teach him anything now it's to have the guts to be true to himself! That's all that matters!

LEAH: Even if he has to betray the whole world to do it?

LYMAN: Only the truth is sacred, Leah!—to hold back nothing!

LEAH: You must be crazy—you hold back everything! You really don't know right from wrong, do you!

LYMAN: Jesus Christ, you sound like Theo!

LEAH: Well maybe it's what happens to people who marry you! Look—I don't think it's a good idea at the moment . . .

LYMAN: I have a right to see my son!

LEAH: I won't have him copying you, Lyman, it will destroy his life! I'm leaving! *She starts to leave.*

LYMAN: You bring me Benny or I'll . . . I'll sue you, god-dammit!

Enter Bessie alone. She is extremely tense and anxious.

BESSIE: Oh, good, I was hoping you'd still be here. Listen . . .

LEAH: I was just going . . .

BESSIE: Oh please wait! My mother's had an attack of some kind . . .

LYMAN: My God, what is it!

BESSIE: They're looking at her in a room down the hall. She's a little delusionary and talks about taking him home with her, and I think it would help for her to see you're still together.

LEAH: But we're not at all together . . .

LYMAN: Wait! Why must it be delusion—maybe she really wants me back!

BESSIE, *with a frustrated stamp of her foot:* I want her out of here and home!

LYMAN: I am not a monster, Bessie! My God, where did all this cruelty come from!

LEAH: He wants her, you see . . .

LYMAN: I want you both!

BESSIE, *a hysterical overtone, screaming:* Will you once in your life think of another human being!

Tom and Theo enter with the Nurse; he has Theo by the arm. She has a heightened, seeing air about her, but a fixed, dead smile, and her head trembles.

LYMAN: Theo!—come, sit her down, Tom!

LEAH, *to Bessie, fearfully:* I really feel I ought to go . . .

THEO: Oh, I wish you could stay for a few minutes! *To Nurse:* Please get a chair for Mrs. Felt.

The reference causes surprise in Bessie. Leah looks quickly to Bessie, perplexed because this is the opposite of what Bessie and Theo wished. Lyman is immensely encouraged. The Nurse, as she goes out for the chair, glances about, perplexed.

Pleasantly: Well! Here we are all together.

Slight pause.

TOM: She's had a little . . . incident, Lyman. *To Bessie:* I've arranged for a plane; the three of us can fly down together.

BESSIE: Oh good. —We're ready to leave whenever you say, Mother.

LYMAN: Thanks, Theo . . . for coming.

THEO, *turns to him, smiling blankly:* Socialism is dead.

LYMAN: Beg your pardon?

THEO: And Christianity is finished, so . . . *Searches* . . . there really is nothing left to . . . to . . . to defend. Except simplicity? *She crosses her legs, and her coat falls partially open, revealing a bare thigh.*

BESSIE: Mother!—where's your skirt?

THEO: I'm comfortable, it's all right . . .

Nurse enters with a chair.

BESSIE: She must have left her skirt in that room she was just in—would you get it, please?

Nurse, perplexed again, exits.

THEO, *to Leah:* I wish I hadn't carried on that way . . . I'm sorry. I've really nothing against you personally, I just never cared for your *type.* The surprise is what threw me, I mean that you were actually married. But I think you are rather an interesting person . . . I was just unprepared, but I'm seeing things much clearer now. Yes. *Breaks off.* Do you see the *Village Voice* up here?

LEAH: Yes, occasionally.

THEO: There was a strange interview some years back with Isaac Bashevis Singer, the novelist? The interviewer was a woman whose husband had left her for another woman, and she couldn't understand why. And Singer said, "Maybe he liked her hole better." I was shocked at the time, really outraged—you know, that he'd gotten a Nobel; but now I think it was courageous to have said that, because it's probably true. Courage . . . courage and directness are always the main thing!

Nurse enters, offers Theo the skirt.

NURSE: Can I help you on with it?

THEO, *takes the skirt, looks at it without recognition, and drops it on the floor:* I can't remember if I called you Leah or Mrs. Felt.

LEAH: I'm not really Mrs. Felt.

THEO, *with a pleasant social smile:* Well, you are *a* Mrs. Felt; perhaps that's all one can hope for when we are so interchangeable—who knows anymore which Mrs. Felt will be coming down for breakfast! *Short pause.* Your boy needs his father, I imagine.

LEAH: Well . . . yes, but . . .

THEO: Then he should be here with you, shouldn't he. We must all be realistic now. *To Lyman:* You can come up here whenever you want to . . . if that's what you'd really like.

BESSIE, *to Tom:* She's really too ill for this. —Come, Mother, we're going.

THEO: I'm not at all ill. *To Lyman:* I can say "fuck," you know. I never cared for the word but I'm sure she has her limitations too. I can say "Fuck me, Lyman," "Fuck you, Lyman"; whatever.

Lyman is silent in guilty anguish.

BESSIE, *to Lyman, furiously:* Will you tell her to leave? Just out of respect, out of friendship!

LYMAN: Yes. *Delicately.* She's right, Theo, I think that would be the best . . .

THEO, *to Bessie:* But I can take better care of him at home. *To Leah:* I really have nothing to do, and you're busy, I imagine . . .

BESSIE: Tom, will you . . .

TOM: Why don't we let her say what's on her mind?

THEO, *to Bessie:* I want to start being real—he had every right to resent me. Truly. What did I ever do but correct him? *To Leah:* You don't correct him, do you. You like him as he is, even now, don't you. And that's the secret, isn't it. *To Lyman:* Well I can do that. I don't need to correct you . . . or pretend to . . .

BESSIE: I can't bear this, Mother!

THEO: But this is our *life,* Bessie dear; you must bear it. —I think I've always pretty well known what he was doing. Somewhere inside we all really know everything, don't we? But one has to live, darling—one has to live . . . in the same house, the same bed. And so one learns to tolerate . . . it's a good thing to tolerate . . . *A furious shout.* And tolerate, and tolerate!

BESSIE, *terrified for her mother:* Daddy, please . . . tell her to go!

LYMAN: But she's telling the truth!

LEAH, *suddenly filling up:* You poor woman! *To him:* What a bastard you are; one honest sentence from you and none of this would have happened, it's despicable! *Appealing to Theo.* I'm so sorry about it, Mrs. Felt . . .

THEO: No-no . . . he's absolutely right—he's always said it—it's life I can't trust! But you—you trust it, and that's why you *should* win out.

LEAH: But it's not true—I never really trusted him! Not really! I always knew there was something dreadful wriggling around underneath! *In full revolt now.* I'll tell you the god-damned truth, I never really wanted to marry anybody! I've ever known one happy couple! —Listen, you mustn't blame yourself, the whole damned thing doesn't work, it never works . . . which I knew and went ahead and did it anyway and I'll never understand why!

LYMAN: Because if you hadn't married me you wouldn't have kept Benny, that's why. *She can't find words.* You wouldn't have had Benny or this last nine years of your happiness. Shit that I am, I helped you become the woman you always wanted to be, instead of . . . *Catches himself.* Well, what's the difference?

LEAH: No, don't stop—instead of what? What did you save me from?

LYMAN, *accepting her challenge:* All right . . . from all those lonely postcoital showerbaths, and the pointless pillow talk and the boxes of heartless condoms beside your bed . . . !

LEAH, *speechless:* Well now!

LYMAN: I'm sick of this crap, Leah! —You got a little something out of this despicable treachery!

THEO: That's a terrible thing to say to the woman.

LYMAN: But the truth is terrible, what else have you just been saying? It's terrible because it's embarrassing, but the truth is always embarrassing or it isn't the truth! —You tolerated me because you loved me, dear, but wasn't it also the good life that I gave you? —Well, what's wrong with that? Aren't women people? Don't people love comfort and power? I don't understand the disgrace here!

BESSIE, *to both women:* Why are you still sitting here, don't you have any pride! *To Leah:* This is disgusting!

LEAH: Will you please stop this high moral tone? I have business with him, so I have to talk to him! —I'll go out of my mind here! Am I being accused of something?

Off to the side, Tom bends his head over clasped hands, eyes shut.

BESSIE: You shouldn't be in the same room with him!

LEAH, *rattled.* I just explained that, didn't I? *What the hell do you want?*

LYMAN, *crying out, voice cracking with a sob:* She wants her father back!

BESSIE: You son of a bitch! *Raises her fists, then weeps helplessly.*

LYMAN: I love you—Bessie!—all of you!

BESSIE: You ought to be killed!

LYMAN: You are all magnificent!

Bessie bursts into tears. A helpless river of grief, which now overflows to sweep up Lyman; then Leah is carried away by the wave of weeping. All strategies collapse as finally Theo is infected. The four of them are helplessly covering their faces. It is a veritable mass keening, a funerary explosion of grief, each for his or her own condition, for love's frustration and for the end of all their capacity to reason. Tom has turned from them, head bent in prayer, hands clasped, eyes shut.

LYMAN, *his eye falls on Theo's bare leg:* Tom, please!—get her to put some clothes on . . . *Breaks off.* Are you praying, for Christ's sake?

TOM, *staring ahead:* There is no way to go forward. You must all stop loving him. You must or he will destroy you. He is an endless string attached to nothing.

LYMAN: Who is not an endless string? Who is sworn to some high golden purpose now—lawyers? Why are you all talking nonsense?

TOM: —Theo needs help now, Lyman, and I don't want a conflict, so I don't see how I can go on representing you.

LYMAN: Of course not, I am not worthy. *A shout, but with the strain of his loss, his inability to connect.* —But I *am* human, and proud of it!—yes, of the glory and the shit! The truth, the truth is holy!

TOM, *exploding:* Is it. Well! Then you'll admit that you moved that barrier aside yourself, and drove onto that sheet of ice? That's the truth, isn't it?

LYMAN, *instant's hesitation:* That was not suicide—I am not a cop-out!

TOM: Why is it a cop-out? Your shame finally caught up with you—or is that too true for comfort? Your shame is the best part of you, for God's sake, why do you pretend you're beyond it? *Breaks off, giving it up.* I'm ready to go, Theo.

LYMAN, *suddenly struck:* One more moment—I beg you all. Before you leave me . . . please. I'd like to tell you something.

BESSIE, *quietly relentless:* Mother?

She raises Theo to her feet. Her head is trembling. She turns to Lyman.

LYMAN: I'm asking you to hear me out, Theo. I see what happened.

THEO: I have nothing left in me anymore, Lyman.

Bessie takes her by the arm to go. Leah stands, as though to leave.

LYMAN: I beg you, Leah, two minutes. I have to tell you this!

LEAH, *an evasive color:* I have work in the office . . .

LYMAN, *losing control:* Two minutes, Leah? Before you take away my son because of my unworthiness? *Pause. Something simple, authentic in his tone stops them all.* Here is how I got on the Mount Morgan road. I kept calling you, Leah, from the Howard Johnson's to tell you I'd be staying over because of the storm . . . but the line was busy. So I went to bed, but it was busy . . . over an hour . . . more! And I started to ask the operator to cut in as an emergency when . . . *Breaks off.* I remembered what you once said to me . . .

LEAH: I was talking to . . .

LYMAN, *in quick fury:* It doesn't matter, I'm not accusing you, or defending myself either, I'm telling you what *happened!*—please let me finish!

LEAH: I was talking to my brother!

LYMAN: In Japan, for over an hour?

LEAH: He just got back on Monday.

LYMAN: Well it doesn't matter!

LEAH: It certainly does matter!

LYMAN: Please let me finish, Leah; remember you once said . . . "I might lie to you," remember that? Way at the beginning? It seemed so wonderful then . . . that you could be so honest; but now, on my back in that room, I started to die.

LEAH: I don't want to hear anymore!

Theo, Bessie are moving out.

LYMAN: Wait! Please! I haven't made my point! *Something new, genuine in his voice stops them.* I want to stop lying. It's simple. *A visionary look.* On my back in that bed, the snow piling up outside . . . the wind howling at my window—this whole nine-year commute suddenly seemed so ludicrous, it was suddenly laughable. I couldn't understand why I'd done it. And somehow I realized that I had no feeling left . . . for myself or anyone . . . I was a corpse on that bed. And I got dressed and drove back into the storm. I don't know— maybe I did want to die, except that what I really thought, Leah . . . was that if I walked in two, three in the morning out of a roaring blizzard like that . . . you'd believe how I needed you. And then I would believe it too, and I'd come back to life again. Unless . . . *Turns to Tom.* I just wanted the end of it all. *To the women:* But I swear to you . . . looking at you now, Theo, and Leah, and you, Bessie . . . I have never felt the love that I feel right now. But I've harmed you and I know it. —And one more thing; I can't leave you with a lie—the truth is that in some miserable, dark corner of my soul I still don't see why I am condemned. I bless you all. *He weeps helplessly.*

Bessie turns Theo to leave.

THEO: . . . Say goodbye to him, dear.

BESSIE, *dry-eyed now; her feeling clearer, she has a close to imper-sonal sound:* I hope you're better soon, Daddy. Goodbye.

She takes her mother's arm—Theo no longer resists as they move out into darkness. He turns to Leah.

LYMAN: Oh Leah, say something tough and honest . . . the way you can.

LEAH: I don't know if I'll ever believe anything . . . or any-body, again.

LYMAN: Oh no. No!—I haven't done that!

A great weeping sweeps Leah and she rushes out.

Leah! Leah! Don't say I've done that!

But she is gone.

TOM: Talk to you soon.

He sees that Lyman is lost in space, and he goes out. The Nurse comes from her corner to Lyman.

NURSE: You got pain?

He doesn't reply.

I'll get you something to smooth you out.

LYMAN: Don't leave me alone, okay?—for a little while? Please, sit with me. *Pats the mattress. She approaches the bed but remains standing.*

I want to thank you, Logan. I won't forget your warmth, especially. A woman's warmth is the last magic, you're a piece of sun. —Tell me . . . when you're out there on the ice with your husband and your boy . . . what do you talk about?

NURSE: . . . Well, let's see . . . this last time we all bought us some shoes at that big Knapp Shoe Outlet up there?— they're seconds, but you can't tell them from new.

LYMAN: So you talked about your new shoes?

NURSE: Well, they're great buys.

LYMAN: Right. That . . . that's just wonderful to do that. I don't know why, but it just is.

NURSE: I'll be right back. *She starts away.*

LYMAN: Hate me?

NURSE, *with an embarrassed shrug:* I don't know. I got to think about it.

LYMAN: Come right back, huh? I'm still a little . . . shaky.

She leans down and kisses his forehead.

Why'd you do that?

NURSE, *shrugs:* No reason.

She exits.

LYMAN, *painful wonder and longing in his face, his eyes wide, alive . . . :* What a miracle everything is! Absolutely everything! . . . Imagine . . . three of them sitting out there together on that lake, talking about their shoes! *He begins to weep, but quickly catches himself.* Now learn loneliness. But cheerfully. Because you earned it, kid, all by yourself. Yes. You have found Lyman at last! So . . . cheer up!

BLACKOUT.